3RD EDITION

Cover Your Assets

Asset Protection
Tax Strategies
Estate Planning

by Jay Butler and
Dr. Robert Hagopian

AssetProtectionServices.com

ISBN 978-0-9914644-2-5

COVER YOUR ASSETS

ASSET PROTECTION • TAX STRATEGIES • ESTATE PLANNING

Table of **Contents**

Disclaimer

The publication is copyrighted © 2016 by Asset Protection Services of America (hereinafter "APSA") with all rights reserved. No part of this publication may be reproduced, retransmitted or rebroadcast in any form or by any means without the express prior written consent of the copyright holder.

Information contained in this publication has been prepared for continuing research and, although these materials may be technical in nature, carries no weight other than being educational in purpose. The materials are provided only as a starting point in order for the reader to undertake his or her own investigation of the subject matter contained herein.

This publication has been garnered from sources deemed reliable at the time of rendering. Since laws, rules, rulings, regulations, statutes and codes are constantly changing and evolving, the information may not be current and APSA takes no responsibility for updating, omitting or correcting any information in this publication.

APSA offers no guarantees the information in this book as being comprehensive, exhaustive, accurate or complete and furthers the information provided is on an "AS IS" basis. Any guidance or reliance on the content found in this publication is at the sole risk of the user. APSA offers no assurances as to the suitability of any particular service or strategy meeting any stated aims, goals or objectives. APSA strongly recommends the reader seek independent accounting, financial, investing, legal, tax or other professional advice.

No representations or warranties are given or implied to render any accounting, financial, investing, legal, tax or other professional advice. No accounting, financial, investing, legal, tax or other professional advice is intended, approved or authorized by APSA. If any accounting, financial, investing, legal, tax or other professional advice is required, then a competent professional should be sought.

APSA and any APSA advisors, directors, employees, members, officers, partners, professional agencies, professional intermediaries, shareholders, staff, ultimate beneficial owners and any other affiliated firms or third-parties wherever situated, take no responsibility whatsoever, whether individually or collectively, for the manner in which the reader may choose to interpret or use the information presented in this publication. APSA shall not be held liable for any civil or criminal liability or damages whether direct, indirect, special or consequential resulting from any interpretations or use of the information provided in this publication.

This publication shall not be taken as sanctioning or advocating any unlawful act or for any improper use of any entity structure, asset protection, tax strategy or estate planning activity, nor for any illegal or fraudulent purposes.

NEVADA TRUSTEE SERVICES GROUP, INC.
Las Vegas Nevada 89128

FOREWORD

After personally writing over 100 books and articles relating to asset protection, wealth preservation and trusts over the last 25 years, I think that I am in a unique position to critically judge when a book hits the mark in explaining in useful easy-to-understand terms the very complexities that is asset protection and asset preservation.

In this third edition of "Cover Your Assets", Jay and I have accomplished just that. In our book, we share with you the product of our collective research, knowledge and experience which we have gained over several decades of personally helping clients achieve their asset protection and wealth preservation goals. Together, we show you step-by-step how to live the "***corporate lifestyle***".

Not only can I unequivocally say that this book is a **MUST READ**, I think it would be a wise addition to anyone's library who wants to learn the secrets that, for so many years, has been religiously hidden from the majority of the population by the wealthy.

Interestingly, if our readers will take the time to read and apply what they will learn in "Cover Your Assets" (3rd Edition), they will have more knowledge about Corporations, LLCs, LPs and Trusts than they will receive by studying business in college.

Dr. [signature]

Dr. Robert Hagopian Msd
Nevada Trustee Service Group, Inc.

Asset Protection Services of America

The inverted "V" displayed on our shield is the uppercase letter "L" in ancient Greek identifying the people of Lacedaemonia, which in historical times was the proper name for the Spartan state. The Greek cry "Molõn Labé" means "Come and Get Them" as spoken by King Leonidas in response to the Persian army's demand for the outnumbered Spartans (300 against 300,000) to surrender their weapons during battle in the narrow pass or 'hot gates' of Thermopylae in 480 B.C. The iconic expression has become a symbol of courage to defend that which belongs to you, even if faced against overwhelming or insurmountable odds.

Author

Jay Butler is the Managing Director of Asset Protection Services of America, the former Managing Director of Asset Protection Services International, Ltd and the former Vice-President of Sales and Marketing for Corporate Support Services of Nevada Inc. Mr. Butler holds a Bachelor's Degree of Fine Arts from Boston University.

Jay has provided customized business entity structuring for clients in all 50 states along with some of the most respected names in the industry including the Jay Mitton organization "the father of asset protection" and Real Estate Investor Association seminars.

While working with Wealth Protection Concepts, LLC under the tutelage of the former Las Vegas and North Las Vegas city attorney Carl E. Lovell Jr. (now deceased from Leukemia), Mr. Butler was bestowed the title of "Asset Protection Planner" for his competency and experience. He also co-authored the first edition of his book "Cover Your Assets: Legal Authorities on Asset Protection, Tax Strategies and Estate Planning" © 2006 with Dr. Lovell.

While residing in Switzerland, Mr. Butler was the Associate Director of "CO-Handelszentrum GmbH" providing Swiss company formation and administration services and executed a full-range of fiduciary responsibilities including sales, client support and international corporate compliance services (KYC, FATCA, AML, FATF and Swiss Code of Obligations).

Jay builds his relationships through consistent attention to detail and reliable support. He has traveled extensively throughout the United States (having visited 49 of the 50 states), explored 36 nations worldwide, and has lived in a total of 7 countries throughout North America, Central America, the Middle East, North Africa and Europe.

Dr Robert Hagopian is semi-retired and the former CEO of Nevada Trustee Services Group Inc, which has provided trustee services to attorneys and law firms throughout the United States since 2005, and the former CEO of the Commerce Bank Ltd in Hong Kong.

Since 1968, Robert has traveled extensively throughout Asia and lived in Japan, Hong Kong and the Philippines with current residency and offices in Manilla.

Dr. Hagopian holds a Bachelor of Science (BS) degree in business administration, an MsD (doctorate) in philosophy and a "jure Dignitatis" Bachelor of Laws degree.

Since 1984, Dr. Hagopian has been structuring business entities for optimum wealth preservation, profitability, asset protection and limiting personal liability through the use of domestic corporations, limited liability companies and various trust vehicles.

Robert has developed innovative processes for the acquisition, holding and marketing of real property. In 2008, Dr. Hagopian applied for the patent-pending "Equity Recovery Program". Based on IRC 351 rules for the transference of real estate to a corporation, the program lawfully avoids capital gains tax, self-employment and state taxes upon the sale of real property.

Contact Us

Please browse our website at www.AssetProtectionServices.com and contact us to schedule your free private asset protection consultation. We welcome the opportunity to hold a 3-way conference call with your tax advisor and/or legal counsel to address any specific questions or concerns you may have. Experience has demonstrated it favorable to have all related parties "on the same page" when creating your structure.

Asset Protection Services of America
701 South Carson Street (Suite #200)
Carson City, Nevada 89701-5239
Office   (775) 461-5255
Skype   Jay_Butler
E-Mail   info@AssetProtectionServices.com
Website   www.AssetProtectionServices.com

Books by Jay Butler and Dr. Robert Hagopian

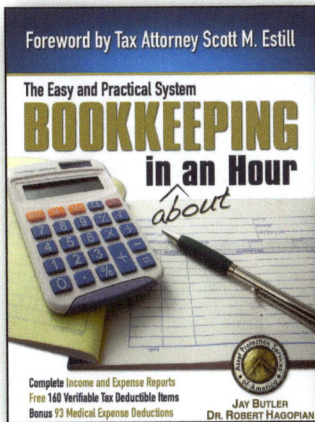

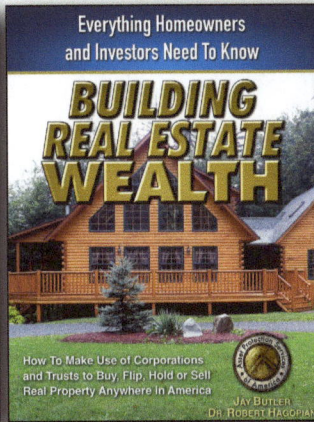

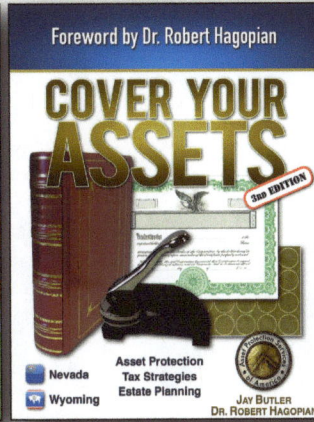

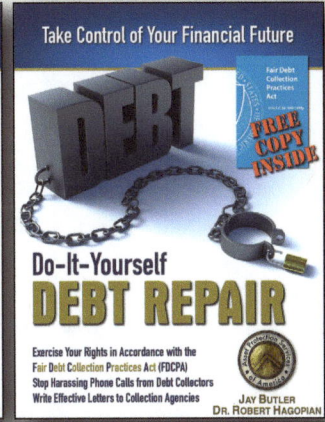

Bookkeeping in About an Hour	ISBN 978-0-9914644-0-1
Building Real Estate Wealth	ISBN 978-0-9914644-1-8
Cover Your Assets *(3rd Edition)*	ISBN 978-0-9914644-2-5
Do-It-Yourself Debt Repair	ISBN 978-0-9914644-7-0

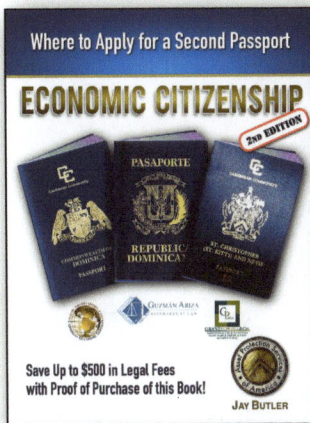

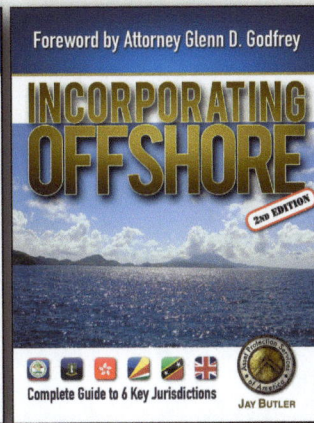

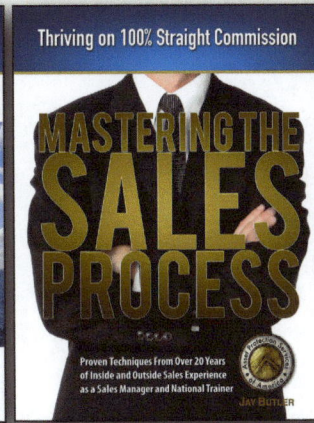

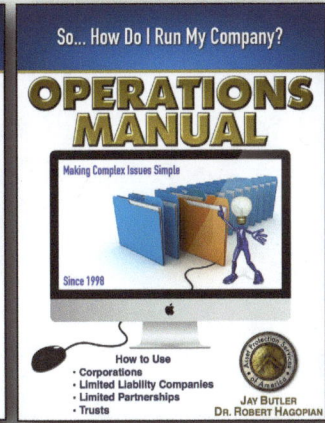

Economic Citizenship *(2nd Edition)*	ISBN 978-0-9914644-4-9
Incorporating Offshore *(2nd Edition)*	ISBN 978-0-9914644-5-6
Mastering the Sales Process	ISBN 978-0-9914644-6-3
Operations Manual	ISBN 978-0-9914644-3-2

Business Solutions

AssetProtectionServices.com

Delaware

Delaware was an excellent state in which to incorporate for decades as they had a non-information sharing agreement with the IRS and did not disclose stock ownership. However Delaware laws changed in 1997 and they have since disclosed stock ownership to the IRS. Delaware has an 8.7% state corporate income tax and may no longer be the best choice of jurisdiction in which to form a private corporation. If you wish to create a corporation that could go public then Delaware may be a good choice as the state arguably has the strongest anti take-over clauses in the nation. On January 26th, 2012 a Federal District Court pierced the veil of a Delaware LLC in the case of *Soroof v. GE*. The egregious ruling did not bode well for the state nor future Delaware LLC members or those who would have otherwise formed an LLC in Delaware.

Nevada

Nevada adopted its statutes for incorporation in 1987 (and revised them again in 2001). The revisions were based on Delaware corporate statutes, but were and taken several steps further. In Nevada, personal liability protection laws are determined by *state statute* and not by judicial determination. Individuals are not subject to case-by-case rulings applied by any one particular judge. Nevada is one of only a dozen states in the country which offers 'series' Limited Liability Companies. Nevada extended the charging order protection as the *exclusive remedy* for a judgment creditor to 'single-member' and 'multi-member' LLC's (as of June 16th 2011) and is the *only* state in America which has extended the charging order protection to qualifying "C" Corporations. Nevada has absolutely no corporate or personal state income tax and no reciprocity agreement with the IRS. Over 95% of all fortune 500 companies are now incorporated in the 'business friendly' state of Nevada.

Wyoming

Wyoming founded the Limited Liability Company in 1977 and is a strong state in which to incorporate. Although Wyoming discloses available stock ownership to the IRS, they don't keep any records on file and therefore have no available information to disclose! It is an ingenious idea and places the low cost of incorporating in Wyoming at the forefront of states in which to incorporate. Wyoming was the *first* state in America to extend the charging order protection as the exclusive remedy for a judgment creditor to a single-member LLC. Wyoming has no broad-based state corporate income tax and no state personal income tax.

Introduction

Many business operators active in this new world economy are discovering the advantages of separating their personal assets from those of their business. Some of the advantages of this separation are greater personal liability protection, tax avoidance and privacy. Unfortunately incorporation laws vary widely throughout the United States and in many states it's so difficult to form a business entity, or the tax laws are so unfavorable, you defeat the purpose of going through the process. However, there are generally no requirements or obligations to incorporate in the state in which you reside. You may go to any of the other states in the union and pick one which best suits your business needs. Whereas Delaware was once the premiere state in which to incorporate, currently Nevada and Wyoming provide the strongest business laws and incorporation benefits of any state in the Union including the lowest rate of taxation and the highest degree of privacy and personal liability protection available.

General Partnerships

A general partnership is a business arrangement in which there is no entity, there is no 'partnership' nor limited partners, but where each partner has managerial power and untitled liability for the debts of the general partnership. A General Partnership is akin to a 'group sole proprietorship and the worst possible environment in which you could find yourself. General Partnerships can be 'automatically determined' to exist in absence of a properly drafted contract / agreement or the formation of an entity filed through the Secretary of State.

Bank Account Introductions

Most new entities can benefit from the opening a corporate bank account. Under such circumstances bank account introductions may be arranged with a local or regional bank representative. A bank account introduction does not guarantee a bank will approve an application to open a corporate bank account as the opening of any account will ultimately depend on the due diligence and business information provided by the client. No influence is exerted on the decision of any bank to accept or decline an application.

With a corporate bank account you can establish a record of income and expense transactions. This is an expected paper trail from any successful business and may be helpful in establishing corporate credit or loans. Upon approval, corporate check books and subsequent banking statements shall be received at your company business address and forwarded to you afterwards to remain in your possession with all other books and records.

Bank Check Disclosures

If you obtain business checks it may be wise to print a disclosure on them. By displaying the **complete entity name**, the **state of incorporation** and **type of entity**, it gives the recipient 'full disclosure' and places the financial liability of the debt instrument onto the entity and, notwithstanding acts of fraud or gross negligence, relieves the signer of individual liability.

My ABC, Corp
(A Nevada Corporation)

My 123, LLC
(A Wyoming Limited Liability Company)

Business Address and Mail Forwarding Services

Any strategy used to protect from an individual from liability, provide anonymity or reduce (or even eliminate) home state taxes requires a physical presence in the state of incorporation. Unless the business entity is 'seated' in the state of incorporation there are discrepancies which state and federal revenue agents may use to challenge your structure. In this computer age, the power and authority of state tax collectors is rivaling that of the IRS. And as agents become more proficient in tax collection, it is imperative to document how your entity meets the requisites of doing business in the state of incorporation.

A physical office, staffed with well-trained personnel (employees) under contract with your entity to serve as the corporate base provides one of the best methods to meet the requirements of 'doing business' in the state of incorporation. But realistically, the logistics of establishing a base of operations can be cost prohibitive and take time and energy away from your current business affairs. The responsibility to locate suitable and affordable office space, negotiate a lease, screen applicants for clerical office positions, train personnel, contend with employee payroll, taxes, insurance, sick leave, vacations and a whole variety of support functions necessary to maintaining an office can be daunting. Individual offices can easily reach $3,000 to $5,000 a month or more for even a small company.

The business location provided for you in Nevada or Wyoming may be used as your official physical and mailing address on advertisements, business cards, envelops, invoices, fliers, letterheads, websites, etc. As mail arrives, it shall be forwarded to you monthly or weekly anywhere within the United States or anywhere in the world. There is a small annual cost, plus shipping and handling fees, to forward all of your mail and packages to an address of your choosing. Such services are available for purchase in addition to your entity formation and are renewable annually.

Business Purpose

All entities must have a Business Purpose and may not be formed solely for tax avoidance.

Confidentiality and Privacy

In Nevada and Wyoming, only the officers and directors of a Corporation, managing members of a Limited Liability Company, and general partners of a Limited Partnership are listed publicly on the Secretary of State website. Nevada and Wyoming do not disclose ownership information publicly or to third parties. Although Wyoming discloses information to the Internal Revenue Service (IRS), it is one of the only states in the Union which does not keep any company records on file. Ownership information is strictly private and therefore its confidentiality is at the discretion of the person whom is in possession of the entity certificates and ledger. In addition to the registered agent, there no ownership information is filed on public record with the Nevada or Wyoming Secretary of State.

Confiscation Provisions

Where any foreign government authority, by way of nationalism, expropriation, confiscation, force or duress, or by imposition of any confiscatory tax, assessment, or other governmental charge, takes or seizes any shares or other interest in a Nevada or Wyoming entity, a Nevada or Wyoming court decision may be obtained ordering the company to disregard the attempted seizure and continue to respect the rights of the Nevada or Wyoming entity owners.

Due Diligence Information

Anti-Money Laundering Acts and Know Your Client (KYC) regulations imposes due diligence obligations upon all financial intermediaries requiring evidence of proof of identity through the form of a color-copy of a government issued ID prior to entering into a business relationship. All orders are required by law to provide Due Diligence Information (DDI).

Employer Identification Number (EIN)

The IRS requires a 'responsible party' provide their Social Security Number to obtain an EIN. *(irs.gov/Businesses/Small-Businesses-&-Self-Employed/Responsible-Parties-and-Nominees)*

Financial Reporting

Nevada and Wyoming entities are required to prepare and file an annual federal income tax return. Nevada and Wyoming entities are free to arrange their business accounts in any manner fitting to establish and maintain reasonable accuracy of the entity's financial position.

Fraudulent Conveyance

A contractual misrepresentation of the nature, quality, or existence of transferred assets. The statute of Fraudulent Conveyance is one year prior to any lawsuit or other problem. Should you transfer assets within one year prior to a lawsuit, the courts and/or government may "unwind" the transfer as though it never happen. The primary 'Badges of Fraud' which generally constitute a fraudulent conveyance include:

1.) Conveyance without Value
2.) Time of Conveyance *(Generally six (6) months to one (1) year prior to a lawsuit)*
3.) Insolvency after Conveyance

Name-Endings

Corporations

Corp	Corporation
Inc	Incorporated
Ltd	Limited
	No Name Ending

Limited Partnerships

LP	Limited Partnership
LLP	Limited Liability Partnership
LLLP	Limited Liability Limited Partnership

Limited Liability Companies

LLC	Limited Liability Company
PLLC	Professional Limited Liability Company

Name Restrictions

The Nevada or Wyoming Secretary of State may, at their own discretion, refuse any entity name which is indecent, offensive or is otherwise objectionable or misleading.

New Company Formations

Corporations, Limited Liability Companies and Limited Partnerships, (also available for Revocable Living Trusts) formed within the United States of America shall, along with their respective documents, receive a records book, customized embossing seal, custom full-color eagle stock certificates / membership interests / partnership interests, gold embossing seals, blank watermarked meeting paper and 'Operations Manual'.

Nominee Services

Nominees for the positions of director, president, secretary, treasurer, manager and general partner have been used in Nevada for over 70 years to take advantage of favorable privacy laws, keeping names and addresses anonymous from prying eyes, solicitors and predatory attorneys. Nevada does not require the disclosure of information about company ownership, stock or capital. Only the director, president, secretary and treasurer of a corporation; the manager of a Limited Liability Company; and general partner of a Limited Partnership are required to be listed on any public record with Secretary of State in Nevada.

There are two types of corporate, company and partnership positions in Nevada, those which are 'public' and those which are 'private'. When an entity is initially created with the Nevada Secretary of State (NV SOS), an 'initial list' is required to be filed displaying the **real names** of those individuals holding positions within the corporation, company or partnership **in order to obtain an EIN and open a bank account**. The positions on this list can be an individual or several people from within the respective entity structure. Either way, this public record will be available for anyone who would have the foreknowledge to request it from the NV SOS.

However, once your name has been removed from the Nevada Secretary of State records and website, generally within a period of only one-to-two days, the NV SOS will not release the information again to anyone unless under court order. Since no one would know at what time your entity is being formed, nor would they have any knowledge of what name for which to search among literally hundreds of thousands of names in the public domain, attorneys could run searches 24 hours a day, 365 days a year, and they would still have no idea what to look for. A potential judgement creditor would have greater odds trying to find the proverbial 'needle in a haystack' than to find your name listed during such a short window of time for an entity whose name is unknown to the public prior to its formation.

The board of directors, managing members or general partners (generally you or an entity you control) can decide to hold a meeting and 'nominate' the leadership positions be changed to another person or 'nominee'. After which time, there are no further bank regulations, IRS mandates or requirements from the State of Nevada to notify the Secretary of State of any additional changes in the actual corporate, company or partnership leadership for the remainder of the (renewal) year. Thus, these 'public' positions can be replaced in 'private' and there are no recorded documents made available as to the actual person(s) holding the current positions.

Utilizing nominee services does not surrender any ownership or control of your corporation, company or partnership. In addition to the respective corporate bylaws, LLC operating agreement and partnership agreement, a carefully drafted 'Declaration of Beneficial Interest' ensures the nominee is striped of any powers. The nominee may hold the public positions of director, officer, president, secretary, treasurer, manager or general partner, but has no authority whatsoever to conduct any business within the respective corporation, company or partnership.

The nominee plays no role at all in any day-to-day operations other than to be listed on the public record. The nominee is not a signer on any bank accounts nor does the nominee have the power to execute any documents on behalf of the corporation, company or partnership.

This 'nominee' formality is understood by the Nevada Secretary of State to be a lawful means of protecting the identity of the leadership. Nominee services are completely legal and commonplace. So, although the names listed on the public record are technically outdated, they remain officially recognized by the state of Nevada as the current standing positions 'held on public record'. The NV SOS requires a new list to be filed annually for the position of director, president, secretary, treasurer, manager and general partner, at which time the process described herein is repeated only the real names of the leadership positions need **NOT** be disclosed again publicly.

Should you need to disclose the officer or director of your corporation to a third party, you can state the position of vice-president as a corporation may have a variety of vice-presidential positions including VP of sales, marketing, manufacturing, warehousing and distribution, etc. And since the position of vice-president is not a position which is reported to the Nevada Secretary of State, the party in question could neither prove nor disprove your stated position.

When an opposing attorney runs an 'asset search' on you as an individual, your position in any corporation, company or partnership utilizing nominee services, you shall remain 'invisible' and your identity as holding any position in a business entity in Nevada would not be detected. Nominee services are a very effective tool at keeping affairs private and defending against attorneys trying to obtain enough information about you to take a case to court.

Nominee Services and the IRS

The Internal Revenue Service regards a nominee as someone who is given limited authority to act on behalf of an entity, usually for a limited period of time, and usually during the formation of the entity. The *"principal officer"* or *"general partner"*, as defined by the IRS, is the true *"responsible party"* for the entity and not a nominee.

When your business applies for its federal tax number, known as an Employer Identification Number (EIN), the entity must disclose the Social Security Number (SSN) for a 'responsible party' of the entity. The IRS defines a responsible party as:

> *" . . . the individual or entity that controls, manages, or directs the entity and the disposition of the entity's funds and assets, unlike a nominee, who is given little or no authority over the entity's assets. The Internal Revenue Service has become aware that nominee individuals are being listed as principal officers and directors, managing members, general partners and/or owners in general in the Employer Identification Number (EIN) application process. **The IRS does not authorize the use of nominees to obtain EINs.**"* (Emphasis Added)

Nominee Services and Legal Opinion

On the 13th of November in 2012, a Nevada attorney named Ms. Gina Bongiovi wrote a well-crafted blog in which she was critical about the way most companies handle their nominee services. Here are some of the key points as addressed in her article:

'Nominee Services and Anonymous Owners'

"Nevada does not provide anonymity for business owners. When you form an entity, you are required to disclose the names of the manager or members if an LLC or officers if a corporation. This information is published on the Nevada Secretary of State's website. Appointing a nominee is dangerous. Here's why:

There is a concept in the law called 'apparent authority' which means a company can be bound by the acts of an agent if the person on the other side of the transaction reasonably believed the agent had the authority to act on the business's behalf.

When you appoint a nominee, they are listed in the public record as, at a minimum, a manager of your company. This means the nominee could sign a contract on behalf of the company and that contract could be enforced because one could reasonably believe that the nominee was authorized to enter into the transaction. It doesn't matter whether the nominee actually had authority; what matters is what an outside person looking at the situation might think.

Therefore, if you're researching the benefits of an 'anonymous LLC' or a nominee service, keep in mind the concept of apparent authority."

– Nevada Attorney, Ms. Gina Bongiovi

While we concur with Ms. Bongiovi in her assessment of nominee services, we have however taken the necessary measures to avoid the legality of problems facing 'apparent authority'. That is, by stating that the person on the public record is a nominee (and by virtue of the declaration of beneficial interest incorporated into our nominee process), we have provided the proper disclosure to avoid any such entanglements. In displaying the name of the nominee, we actually name them as "Nominee" on the Nevada Secretary of State public record. Divulging the status of the respective leadership position as such absolutely resolves the problem articulated by Ms. Bongiovi while simultaneously providing the privacy protection and anonymity that only a properly structured nominee service provider can offer.

Paid Up Capital

Nevada and Wyoming entities are not required to have any paid-up capital in order to initiate business operations.

Resident Agent and Registered Office Requirements

State laws require that all business entities retain the services of a 'resident agent' and 'registered office' for the service of process (a lawsuit) and any government notices. In the event an entity is ever sued, the lawsuit would be delivered to the resident agent who, in-turn, would overnight such documents directly to you anywhere in the world. The resident agent is required to have on file a copy of the initial filing documents and the name and address of the person who retains the ownership record ledger, but the resident agent is not required to possess the original filing documents nor the ledger itself. Every business entity formed is required to have resident agent and registered office services for a period of one-year renewable on an annual basis in accordance with State law.

State Business Licenses and Fees

Obtaining and maintaining a Nevada Business License is a requirement under the Nevada Revised Statutes in Chapter 76 - "State Business Licenses". With few exceptions, Nevada entities are subject to a $200 Nevada state business license ("For Profit" Corporations are $500). Thus bringing the total annual Secretary of State renewal fees to $325 - $625 per entity with the $150 fee for the annual list of officers and directors. Should you ever be audited, a Nevada state business license is an item your state or federal tax authorities will undoubtedly wish to see as it is a critical document toward validating your entity to be a genuine and fully functioning business in the state of Nevada. Entities which fall outside the scope of the Nevada State Business License can be found in the Nevada Revised Statutes (NRS) under Section 76.020 which includes, among other things, businesses organized pursuant to NRS Chapter 82 or 84 (non-profit Corporations filing an 1120 or 1120-S). Wyoming has no State Business License requirements, but has a $50 annual filing fee.

Structuring

Nevada and Wyoming entities have independent legal personalities and possess the same powers as a natural person.

Taxation

Nevada and Wyoming have no state corporate income tax but, as with all states, may be subject to federal company income tax on any earnings.

Tandem Flow-Chart

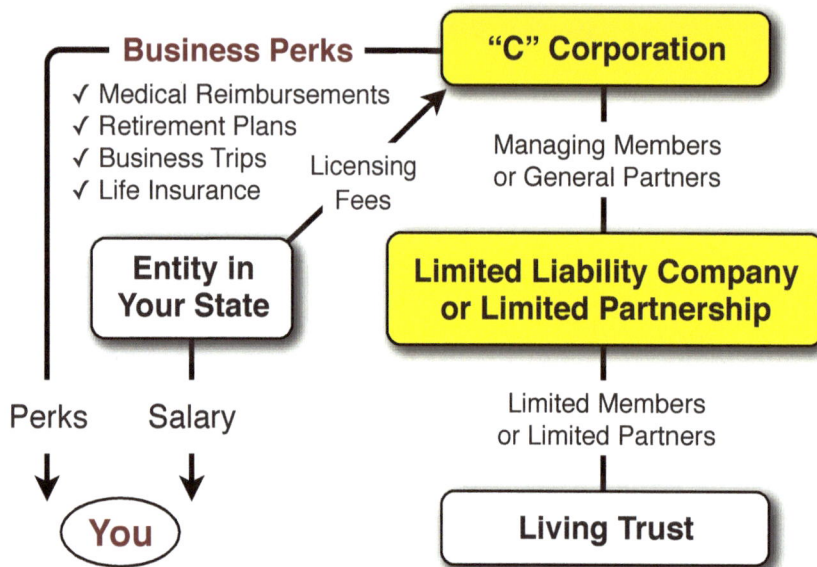

Business Perks
- ✓ Medical Reimbursements
- ✓ Retirement Plans
- ✓ Business Trips
- ✓ Life Insurance

Licensing Fees

"C" Corporation

Nevada "C" Corporation
- ✓ Charging Order Protection
- ✓ No IRS Reciprocity Agreement
- ✓ Shareholders Not Public Record
- ✓ Officers & Directors Public Record
- ✓ Nominee Services Available
- ✓ No State Corporate Income Tax

Entity in Your State

Managing Members or General Partners

Limited Liability Company or Limited Partnership

Nevada LLC and LP
- ✓ Charging Order Protection
- ✓ No IRS Reciprocity Agreement
- ✓ LLC Limited Members and LP Limited Partners Not Public Record
- ✓ LLC Managing Members and LP General Partners Public Record
- ✓ Nominee Services Available
- ✓ No State Corporate Income Tax

Perks   Salary

You

Limited Members or Limited Partners

Living Trust

Helpful Definitions

Articles of Incorporation / Organization

A formal document (also known as a 'Charter') that creates a Corp / LLC / LP.

Board of Directors

A group of persons elected by shareholders to oversee the management of a Corporation.

ByLaws / Operating Agreement / Partnership Agreement

Rules adopted by an organization chiefly for the government of its shareholders / members / partners and the regulation of its affairs; the internal rules and regulations of an organization.

Certificate of Filing

A Certificate of Filing comes from the Secretary of State showing evidence that on a specific date the Articles of Incorporation / Organization were filed with an approved state authority.

Directors / Managing Members / General Partners

Persons elected by the shareholders / members / partners to oversee the entity management.

Writing-Off
Business Start-Up Costs

Under the Internal Revenue Service Publication 535, Section 8 Amortization, in the subsection on Starting a Business, the following Business Start-Up Costs are defined as deductible capital expenses that are used to pay for:

(a) creating an active trade or business; or

This includes costs incurred for surveying markets, product analysis, labor supply, visiting potential business locations or related expenditures.

(b) investigating the creation or acquisition of an active trade or business.

This includes costs for employee training and wages, consultant fees, advertising and travel costs associated with finding suppliers, distributors, and customers. Such expenses can only be claimed if your research or investigation ends with the formation of a successful business.

Costs of Organizing a Corporation, Limited Liability Company or Limited Partnership
For the creation of an entity, including such organizational costs as:
- *the cost of temporary directors;*
- *the cost of organizational meetings;*
- *accounting fees for services incident to the organization;*
- *State incorporation fees;*
- *the cost of legal services.*

These costs must have been incurred before the end of your first tax year in business. They must also be chargeable to a capital account and amortized over the life of the Corporation, Limited Liability Company or Limited Partnership.

If you started your business in 2011 or later with start-up costs of $50,000 or less, you can deduct up to $5,000 in business startup costs on your tax return.

Restrictions apply on start-up costs exceeding $50,000 and can be wiped-out altogether if the aggregate amount exceeds $55,000. Such tax planning exceeds the scope of this information and a tax advisor should be sought on how to capitalize or amortize such expenses if you anticipate first-year start-up costs exceeding $55,000.

About Nevada

SECRETARY OF STATE

STATE OF NEVADA

Why Incorporate in Nevada?

No Gift Tax
No Estate Tax
No Luxury Tax
No Unitary Tax
No Franchise Tax
No Inheritance Tax
No Capital Gains Tax
No Personal Income Tax
No Corporate Income Tax
No Tax on Corporate Shares
Nominee Services Permitted
Nominal Annual State Filing Fees
No Reciprocity Agreement with the IRS
No Minimum Capital Start-Up Requirements
Stockholders are Not a Matter of Public Record

About Nevada

Activities

Death Valley is a 13,630 square kilometer (Km2) national park drawing over 800,000 visitors annually. Large professional cycling attractions have recently been preserved including an "epic ride" inside Bootleg Canyon Mountain Bike Park. The Sierra Nevada Mountains offer Olympic skiing, snowmobiling and back-country snowshoeing. Lake Tahoe provides ice skating and ice fishing in the winter, sailing, kayaking and even scuba diving in the summer. Mount Charleston offers year-round access for Las Vegas residents and guests to hiking trails and a modest ski resort. Three desert ecosystems feed into Lake Mead at the Hoover Dam creating a natural resort destination for boaters and fisherman.

Climate

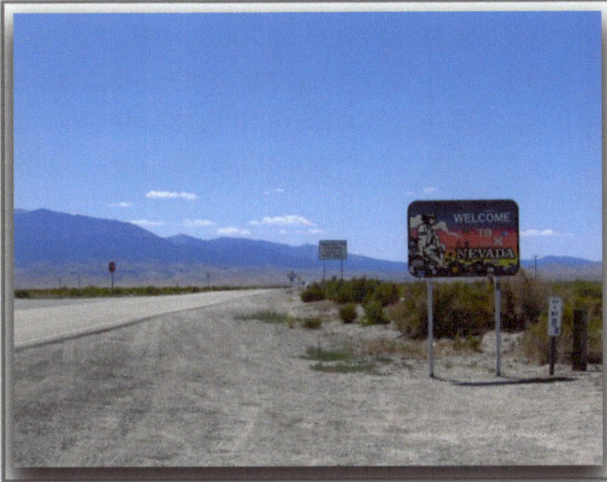

Nevada is mostly a semiarid desert climate with low humidity. Summer temperatures are generally over 40°C and often reach in excess of 50°C in the central and southern regions of the state. Winters are mild, but go below -40°C in the mountains. Annual rainfall is quite low statewide at only 18 cm, with the some of the mountains seeing as much as 1 meter.

Culture

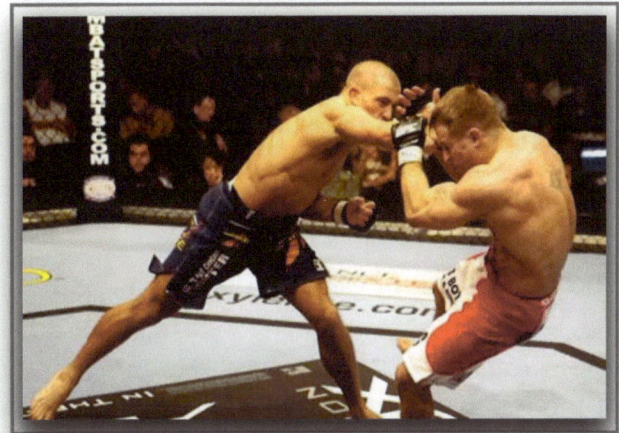

Established in 1905, Las Vegas is the 28th most populous city in the United States and considered the epicenter of Nevada. Famous for its Friday night fights, high-end casinos, luxury resorts, shopping, fine dining, spectacular shows, adult entertainment, clubs and spas, Vegas is justifiably coined the "Entertainment Capital of the World". Performers from across the globe debut in Vegas and numerous Hollywood films and television shows have been filmed on the 6.8 kilometer stretch of Las Vegas Boulevard known as "The Strip". Most Nevadans immigrated from Utah and more recently California. Nevada has a 3.5% annual growth rate and natives often feel "Californicated" due to the influx of Californians.

Economy and Financial Services

Agricultural commodities include cattle, hay, alfalfa, dairy, onions and potatoes. Industrial commodities include tourism, mining, minerals, machinery, printing, publishing, food processing and electric equipment. In 2007, Nevada produced $127 Billion with gaming and gaming related revenue sustaining $25 Billion, or 1/5th of the state total. The Silver State was responsible for producing over 160 metric tons of gold in 2009, which is 80% of the annual gold production in the United States and 10% of the world's annual gold production. Nevada has a minimum statewide sales tax rate of 6.85% and may accompany a county sales tax reaching a combined high of 8.1% as is the case in Clark county. Nevada is the only state in the union which has no personal income tax, no corporate income tax and no reciprocity agreement with the Internal Revenue Service (IRS). Asset Protection Services of America offers incorporation services for Corporations, Land Trusts, Limited Liability Companies, and Living Trusts in the United States of America.

The great state of Nevada derives its name from the Spanish word meaning "snow covered" and refers to the Sierra "Nevada" Mountains. Most of the state is part of a 28,000 square kilometer great basin extending into California, Oregon, Idaho and Utah. Nevada has 172 mountain summits, second most in the United States only to Alaska. Many of these mountains have peaks exceeding 4,000 meters with valleys at altitudes above 3,000 meters. Outside of Reno, the northern two-thirds of Nevada are sparsely populated; even US Highway 50 has been named the "Loneliest Road in America". The lower third of the state is situated within the Mojave Desert and home to over 2 Million people.

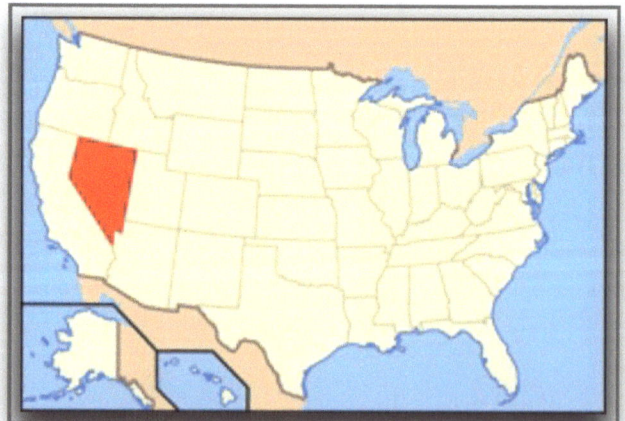

Geography

History

Nevada is known as the "Silver State" for the first major silver discovery in the United States back in 1858. Unregulated gaming was outlawed in 1909 and remained in effect for decades until March of 1931 when the legislature reinstated it just in time for construction on one of the largest projects in American history. The Hoover Dam, formerly the Boulder Dam, was a concrete arch-gravity damn built between 1931 and 1935 during the great depression. The dam is located about 40 kilometers southeast of Las Vegas in the Black Canyon of the Colorado River along the Nevada and Arizona border. The enormity of the project and lack of local resources and facilities near the site drove business into the region to support over 5,000 workers and the nearly 20,000 men and their families vying for those positions. After completion many of the workers joined the United States military particularly after the onset of World War II. Through Benjamin "Bugsy" Siegel, Las Vegas soon became a hot spot destination for legalized gaming and adult entertainment.

Capital	Population
Carson City	2,723,322
Official Language	GDP
English	$128 Billion
Government	Currency
Republic	United States Dollar
Laws	Driving
Common Law	Right
Independence Day	Internet
October 31st, 1864	.us
Total Area	Calling Code
286,367 Km2	+1 (702)

Interesting Facts

About Wyoming

About Wyoming

Activities

Wyoming is home to landmarks like Yellowstone National Park, Bighorn Canyon, Devil's Tower, Flaming Gorge, Fossil Butte, and the Grand Tetons. There's a veritable plethora of outdoor activities in which to partake including; art and music festivals, bird watching, boating, canoeing, caving, dogsledding, fly fishing, ghost town tours, gold panning, golfing, hiking, historical sites, horseback riding, horseshoeing, hot air ballooning, hot spring bathing, hunting, kayaking, rafting, rock climbing, rodeo attractions, skiing, sleigh rides, snowboarding, snowmobiling, spas, wagon train rides, and wildlife refuges, to name a few.

Climate

As a semi-arid continental state, Wyoming experiences dry and windy conditions with extreme temperature changes. Summers days average 29°C with cooler summer evenings dropping down to only 13°C. Wyoming winters have the potential to be long and foreboding with temperatures hovering between 9°C to -7°C during the day and -18°C or more at night from December through February. Most of the state sees very little precipitation (less than 25 cm), but the mountain ranges may accumulate over 50 cm, most of which is snow.

Culture

Wyoming is the 10th largest territory in the Union, the second least densely populated state, and the least populous state in America. Wyomingites are a rugged, self-reliant, outdoor people who love their freedom and right to bear arms. According to the United States Census Bureau, over 86% of the state is comprised of (non-Hispanic) white people. About 9% of the state is made of Hispanic or Latino origin, 2.5% consists of various native americans, with the balance being a mix of Alaskans, Asians, Hawaiians, and Pacific Islanders. Almost 80% of the population considers themselves Christians and more than half of those are of the Protestant denomination.

Economy and Financial Services

Mineral extraction, along with travel and tourism are the economic backbone of Wyoming. Total taxable mining production exceeds $8 Billion and tourism accounts for over $2.5 Billion in state revenue. The Federal government owns roughly 50% of Wyoming's land mass, and more than 2.5 million people visit Wyoming's national parks and monuments annually. Agricultural commodities produced in Wyoming include grain (wheat and barley), hay, livestock (beef), sugar beets, and wool. Wyoming has no state personal income tax and no broad-based corporate income tax. Asset Protection Services of America offers incorporation services for Corporations, Land Trusts, Limited Liability Companies, and Living Trusts in the United States of America.

Geography

The northern Wyoming border is situated halfway between the equator and the north pole at the 45° latitude. Interestingly enough, Wyoming is one of only three states (along with Colorado and Utah) to have straight latitudinal and longitudinal lines with no naturally defined borders. Nearly two-thirds of Wyoming is a high desert great plains, most of which is in excess of 1,500 meters in altitude. The highest point in Wyoming is Gannett Peak in the Wind River Mountain Range at 4,207 meters with the second highest point being in the famous Grand Tetons. Other ranges include the Bighorn Mountain Range which run through the central northern part of the state, the Rocky Mountains to the west, and the Snowy Range to the south. The continental divide runs through Wyoming as do numerous rivers including the Bighorn, Cheyenne, Green, North Platte, Snake and Yellowstone.

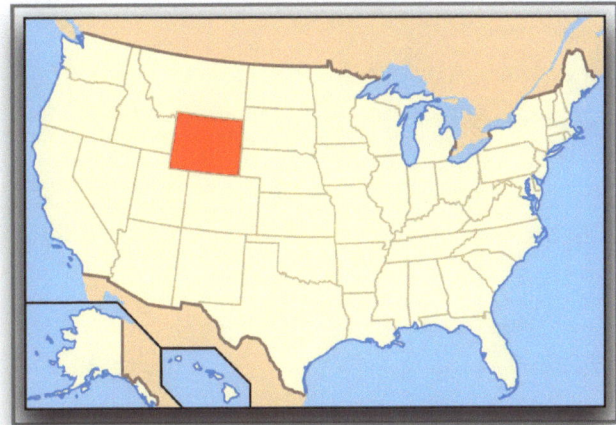

History

The Arapahoe, Crow, Lakota, and Shoshone were among some of the original Wyoming Native American inhabitants. Southern portions of Wyoming were once part of the Spanish Empire and Mexican Territories. The first explorers to provide account of the land and natural resources arrived in 1807. It wasn't until 1848 that Wyoming was ceded to the United States at the conclusion of the Mexican - American War. Following many of the routes used in the Oregon Trail, both the Pacific Railroad and Highway 80 were constructed across Wyoming in 1868 and operate to this today. Yellowstone became the world's first National Park in 1872 and in 1869 Wyoming was the first state in the Union to extend the right to vote to women. Known as the 'state of equality', Wyoming is also known for having the first female juror, court bailiff, justice of the peace, and governor. Wyoming lead the United States with the founding of Limited Liability Companies in 1977.

Capital Cheyenne	**Population** 568,158
Official Language English	**GDP** $38 Billion
Government Republic	**Currency** United States Dollar
Laws Common Law	**Driving** Right
Independence Day July 10th, 1890	**Internet** .us
Total Area 253,348 Km2	**Calling Code** +1 (307)

Interesting Facts

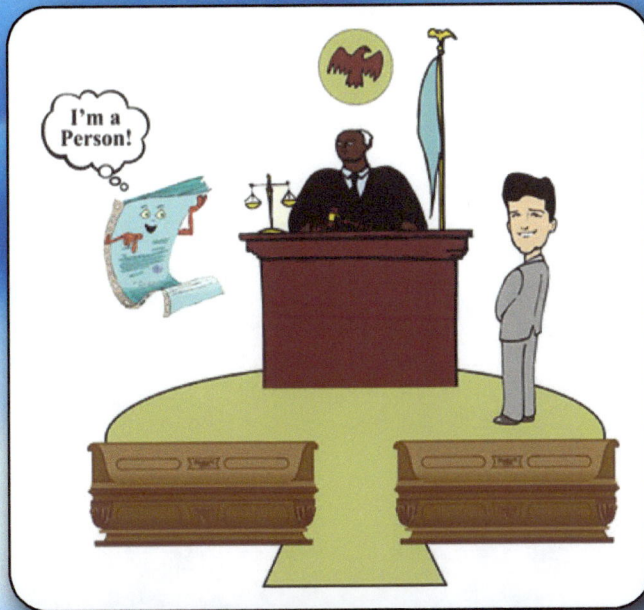

What is an Entity?

AssetProtectionServices.com

What is an Entity?

An entity is a person, and Black's law dictionary defines a "Person" as:

1.) **A Human Being**;
2.) **An Entity** *(such as a corporation or limited liability company) that is recognized by law as having the rights and duties of a human being.*

So if you were standing in front of a judge and there was an entity (a piece of paper) and you (the human being), both are recognized by the court as a person.

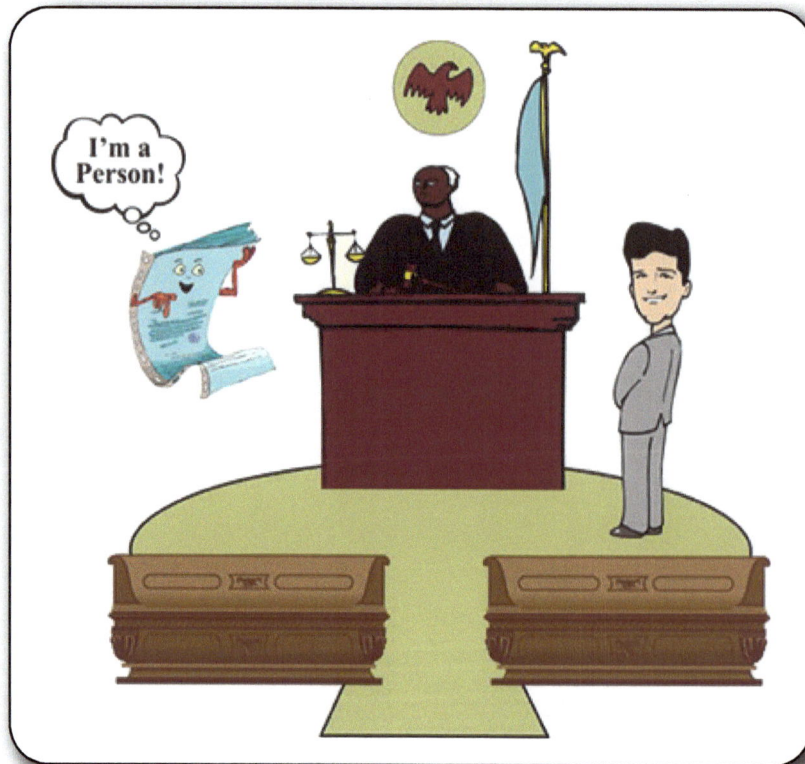

Never Bring the Pain Home

Any assets held directly in your name, or that of a revocable trust, are subject to seizure by a judgement creditor. Assets properly held in the name of an entity are *not* subject to the same.

Imagine if a person were sentenced to be burned at the stake. Would you prefer that 'person' be you (a flesh and blood human being) or an 'entity' like a corporation (a piece of paper or 'fictional' person). I'd imagine you would prefer the entity get torched and not you!

As John D. Rockefeller famously said, "Own nothing, control everything."

Charging Order Protection

What is Charging Order Protection?

"A right is only as great as its remedy." - Legal Maxim

Charging Order Protected Entity (COPE) is the term used to describe entities for which judgment creditors are limited to the charging order protection remedy. A Charging Order is the *remedy* a creditor uses to place a judgment against a Limited Liability Company, Limited Partnership or a qualifying (Nevada) Corporation which, ironically, becomes the primary *defense* for the respective members, limited partners or shareholders.

Judges may award creditors the *rights* of an assignee (distribution of profits) but not the membership, partnership or shareholder *interests* of an assignee (ownership). These "transferee rights" do not grant creditors any control or ability to participate in the management of the company. As such, creditors have no say as to when, and in what amount, distributions can be made. The judgement creditor may *not* force distributions, nor maintain managerial rights or exercise any measure of control over the Limited Liability Company, Limited Partnership or Corporation. The charging order protects investors from the judgment creditors of a debtor owner.

If it weren't for the asset protection afforded to a Limited Liability Company, Limited Partnership and (Nevada) Corporation through the 'Charging Order Protection', investors would not have the confidence currently enjoyed when participating in business activities within the United States.   Members, partners or shareholders should not fear being held hostage by the debts of another member, partner or shareholder, thus it is equally important for members, partners and shareholders to have their interests and legal rights protected. But not all states offer equal charging order protection. In addition to Nevada and Wyoming, there are only a handful of states which permit a court to grant the charging order protection as the *exclusive* or *sole* remedy to a judgment creditor, including Arizona, Arkansas, Delaware, Connecticut, Idaho, Illinois. Louisiana, Maryland, Minnesota, Oklahoma, Rhode Islands and Virginia.

Capital Contribution Limitations

The members in a Limited Liability Company, the (limited) partners in a Limited Partnership and shareholders in a (Nevada) Corporation are *not* individually liable for the debts and obligations of the company or partnership. Members, partner and shareholder liabilities are limited to their respective capital contribution to the company, partnership or corporation. Nevada and Wyoming are unique among a handful of states which extend such capital contribution limitations to 'single-member' LLC's.

Charging Order Protection Origins

The charging order came into existence under the 1914 passage of the Uniform Partnership Act (or "UPA"). And although the legislation was the preferred judicial remedy for limited partnerships (at the time), it lead to an unintended consequence for other partners in that a judgement creditor could force the seizure of partnerships assets, sell the debtor-partner's interests in those assets causing the 'compulsory dissolution and winding up' of the partnership. Such a 'remedy' hardly seemed fair to the innocent partners whose financial affairs were in order and separate from those of the partnership, particularly when such judgement creditors could elect to step into the shoes of the debtor-partner and compel the remaining partners to participate in the partnership involuntarily.

This 'forced partnership' was found to be at odds with the principle of *delectus personae*, or the idea that partnerships (as well as limited liability companies and corporations) are *"at their core . . . relations of trust between partners"* and that *"when personal relationship are important, a person cannot be compelled to associate with another person."*

To prevent creditors from compelling such forced associations and dissolutions of a partnership, later versions of the UPA (such as the Uniform Limited Partnership Act "ULPA" and the Uniform Limited Liability Company Act "ULLCA") restricted creditor remedies to the charging order by stating *"partnership property is not subject to attachment or execution"* and appointing *"receivers"* to keep creditors of debtor-partners from usurping the debtor's position as partner.

However, with the introduction of single-member limited liability companies, the question arose as to what would happen when there were no other member interests to protect? The question was answered quite bluntly in the federal bankruptcy case of Ashley Albright.

Ashley Albright
Colorado

The courts often consider an LLC with a single-member to be the liable party, as did Colorado in the 2003 bankruptcy case of Ashley Albright wherein the court stated:

> "A charging order protects the autonomy of the original members and their ability to manage their own enterprise. In a single-member entity, there are no non-debtor members to protect. The charging order limitation serves no purpose in a single member limited liability company, because there are no other parties' interests affected." [Ashley Albright, Case No. 01-11367, 291 B.R. 538 (Bankr. D Colo. 2003)]

The court granted full economic and non-economic rights to the bankruptcy trustee, allowing the bankruptcy trustee to manage the debtor's LLC. The trustee subsequently sold the LLC's property and distributed the net proceeds to the bankruptcy estate for satisfaction of creditors' claims. Other states have concurred with this ruling as did California district courts in the cases of [*Crocker National Bank v. Perroton, (208 Cal. App. 3d 1, 1989)*], and [*Hellman v. Anderson, (233 Cal. App. 3d 840, 1991)*]. More egregious is that these cases set the precedent for other California judges, who rule not by state statute but by judicial determination, and other courts nationwide to build onerous case law. Thus, single-member LLC's have no assurance of liability protection in most states throughout the Union. However Nevada and Wyoming legislation still afford a single-member LLC charging order protection in writing under Nevada Revised Statutes section 86 and Wyoming Title 17.

Olmstead v. FTC
Florida

In June of 2010, the Florida Supreme Court heard the case of Olmstead v. Federal Trade Commission (FTC) and determined the charging order was intended to protect *other* members from creditors intruding into the business affairs of the LLC. A dissenting judge said:

> *"[T]he principles used to ignore the LLC statutory language under the current factual circumstances apply with equal force to multimember LLC entities and, in essence, today's decision crushes a very important element for all LLCs in Florida. If the remedies available under the LLC Act do not apply here because the phrase "exclusive remedy" is not present, the same theories apply to multimember LLCs and render the assets of all LLCs vulnerable. [Olmstead, et. al., vs. Federal Trade Commission, Supreme Court of Florida. Case No. SC08-1009 (June 24, 2010)]*

Florida ruled that a single-member LLC membership interest *is* subject to seizure by a creditor in the same manner as corporate stock. Therefore a creditor of a Florida single-member LLC is permitted to seize a membership interest. Concerned with the implications of this ruling on 'multi-member' LLC protection, Florida amended their laws in 2011 to afford 'multi-member' LLC's charging order protection. Although Nevada and Wyoming statutes remain intact, more states may soon adhere to Florida's ruling on single-member LLC entities.

Soroof v. GE
Delaware

On January 24th, 2012 a Federal District Court pierced the veil of a Delaware LLC in the case of *Soroof v. GE* [Soroof Trading Development Company, Ltd vs. GE Fuel Cell Systems, LLC No. 10 Civ. 1391(LTS)(JCF), 2012 WL 209110 (S.D.N.Y. Jan. 24. 2012)] without even explaining how the Delaware requirement of 'unfairness' or 'injustice' was met. The court, which had dismissed claims that the LLC had improperly filed a 'Certificate of Cancellation', should have also dismissed the veil piercing claims against the LLC members. Piercing the veil is not an independent cause of action but a method of imposing liability on an underlying claim, and there were no other other underlying claims in the case to impose such a liability. Piercing the veil is an equitable remedy, not a cause of action unto itself. Such egregious rulings do not bode well for Delaware, nor for the future of Delaware LLC members.

Charging Order Protection Circumvention

The most important aspects to avoid the charging order protection being circumvented are as follows, in order of importance:

1.) The entity is a single-member Limited Liability Company;
2.) The operating agreement, partnership agreement or articles of organization are non-executory in nature (applicable only in bankruptcy proceedings);
3.) The forfeiture of a debtor's membership interest to a creditor would not interrupt the company, partnership or corporation business;
4.) All members, partners, shareholders of the entity become a debtor of the same creditor.

Executory in Nature

To ensure the operating agreement, partnership agreement or articles of organization are executory in nature, there are several ingredients for which to look in the drafting of the respective document. The court case of *[Ehmann (2005 WL 78921 (Bankr. D. Ariz. 2005)]* demonstrated that an LLC operating agreement is executory when members have the following on-going obligations to:

1.) contribute cash to the entity;
2.) contribute non-managerial services to the entity;
3.) contribute equipment or other property to the entity; and/or
4.) manage the entity.

Participation, Obligations and Consultations

A few ways to meet these these requirements is to ensure every member, partner or shareholder to do one or more of the following:

Active Participation – Have a written agreement to act as the managing member, general partner or managing director as long as he or she holds a membership interest, partnership interest or stock ownership in the Limited Liability Company, Limited Partnership or Corporation respectively, as a condition of such continued membership or ownership.

Non-Transferrable Obligations – Additionally, the operating agreement of Limited Liability Company (LLC), the partnership agreement of a Limited Partnership (LP) and the articles of organization for a Corporation (Corp) should stipulate that managing members, general partners or managing directors, unless incapacitated, cannot transfer their obligations while they remain with the Limited Liability Company, Limited Partnership or Corporation due to the fact that their intimate involvement with company affairs uniquely qualifies them to know how to best advise or manage the company.

Passive Consultations – A non-managing member, partner or stockholder should agree to act in a passive advisory or consulting role to the company as long as he is a member or owner, as a condition of such continued membership or ownership. These services should be demonstrable in court and could include such activities as submitting an annual report to the company giving recommendations as to how the company could increase its profits and become more efficient. Such a report could then be submitted to the court as proof on-going executory obligations are being performed.

<h3 align="center">Separating Liability</h3>

Never, under any circumstances, should all members of a Limited Liability Company, Limited Partnership or Corporation personally become debtors of the same creditor. This can be avoided by following any one or more of the following methods:

1.) Ensure at least one of the members, partners or shareholders is never exposed to liability. This may be accomplished by making one of the members, partners or shareholders a trust or other entity that only engages in "safe" activities and incurs no debt; and/or

2.) Make sure that at least one member, partner or shareholder is not an insider or affiliate of another member, partner or shareholder under the Uniform Fraudulent Transfer Act "UFTA".

Charging Order Protection
Nevada

On June 16th, 2011 Nevada Senate Bill 405 passed and amended the Nevada Revised Statute 78.746, which subsequently was enacted and became law on October 1st 2011, to specifically provide Nevada "C" Corporations charging order protection as the *exclusive remedy* for a judgement creditor. The great state of Nevada is currently the **only** state in the union to provide charging order protection to a Corporation.

Corporation
Nevada Revised Statute (NRS)
Section 78 - Private Corporations
NRS 78.746 - Action Against Stockholder by Judgement Creditor; Limitation
(Added to NRS by 2007, 2639; A 2009, 2829)

1. *On application to a court of competent jurisdiction by a judgment creditor of a stockholder, the court may charge the stockholder's stock with payment of the unsatisfied amount of the judgment with interest. To the extent so charged, the judgment creditor has only the rights of an assignee of the stockholder's stock.*

2. *This section:*
  (a) *Applies only to a corporation that:*
      (1) *Has more than 1 but fewer than 100 stockholders of record at any time.*
      (2) *Is not a subsidiary of a publicly traded corporation, either in whole or in part.*
      (3) *Is not a professional corporation as defined in NRS 89.020.*
  (b) *Does not apply to any liability of a stockholder that exists as the result of an action filed before July 1, 2007.*
  (c) *Provides the exclusive remedy by which a judgment creditor of a stockholder or an assignee of a stockholder may satisfy a judgment out of the stockholder's stock of the corporation.*
  (d) *Does not deprive any stockholder of the benefit of any exemption applicable to the stockholder's stock.*
  (e) *Does not supersede any private agreement between a stockholder and a creditor if the private agreement does not conflict with the corporation's articles of incorporation, bylaws or any shareholder agreement to which the stockholder is a party.*

3. *As used in this section, "rights of an assignee" means the rights to receive the share of the distributions or dividends paid by the corporation to which the judgment debtor would otherwise be entitled. The term does not include the rights to participate in the management of the business or affairs of the corporation or to become a director of the corporation.*

Charging Order Protection
Nevada

Limited Liability Company
Nevada Revised Statutes (NRS)
Section 86 - Limited Liability Companies
NRS 86.401 - Rights and remedies of creditor of member.
(Added to NRS by 1991, 1302; A 2001, 1393, 3199; 2003, 20th Special Session, 71; 2011, 2800)

1. *On application to a court of competent jurisdiction by any judgment creditor of a member, the court may charge the member's interest with payment of the unsatisfied amount of the judgment with interest. To the extent so charged, the judgment creditor has only the rights of an assignee of the member's interest.*

2. *This section:*

(a) *Provides the exclusive remedy by which a judgment creditor of a member or an assignee of a member may satisfy a judgment out of the member's interest of the judgment debtor, whether the limited-liability company has one member or more than one member. No other remedy, including, without limitation, foreclosure on the member's interest or a court order for directions, accounts and inquiries that the debtor or member might have made, is available to the judgment creditor attempting to satisfy the judgment out of the judgment debtor's interest in the limited-liability company, and no other remedy may be ordered by a court.*

(b) *Does not deprive any member of the benefit of any exemption applicable to his or her interest.*

(c) *Does not supersede any written agreement between a member and a creditor if the written agreement does not conflict with the limited-liability company's articles of organization or operating agreement.*

Charging Order Protection
Nevada

Limited Partnership
Nevada Revised Statutes (NRS)
Section 88 - Uniform Limited Partnership Act
NRS Section 88.535 - Rights and Remedies of Creditor of Partner
(Added to NRS by 1985, 1290; A 2001, 1400, 3199; 2003, 3155; 2003, 20th Special Session, 101; 2011, 2807)

1. *On application to a court of competent jurisdiction by any judgment creditor of a partner, the court may charge the partnership interest of the partner with payment of the unsatisfied amount of the judgment with interest. To the extent so charged, the judgment creditor has only the rights of an assignee of the partnership interest.*

2. *This section:*
   (a) *Provides the exclusive remedy by which a judgment creditor of a partner or an assignee of a partner may satisfy a judgment out of the partnership interest of the judgment debtor. No other remedy, including, without limitation, foreclosure on the partner's partnership interest or a court order for directions, accounts and inquiries that the debtor or partner might have made, is available to the judgment creditor attempting to satisfy the judgment out of the judgment debtor's interest in the limited partnership, and no other remedy may be ordered by a court.*
   (b) *Does not deprive any partner of the benefit of any exemption laws applicable to the partnership interest of the partner.*
   (c) *Does not supersede any written agreement between a partner and creditor if the written agreement does not conflict with the partnership's certificate of limited partnership or partnership agreement.*

Charging Order Protection
Wyoming

Limited Liability Company
Wyoming Title 17
Chapter 29 - Wyoming Limited Liability Act
Article 5 - Transferable Interests and Rights of Transferees and Creditors
Section 503 - Charging Order

(a) *On application by a judgment creditor of a member or transferee, a court may enter a charging order against the transferable interest of the judgment debtor for the unsatisfied amount of the judgment. A charging order requires the limited liability company to pay over to the person to which the charging order was issued any distribution that would otherwise be paid to the judgment debtor.*

(b) *Reserved.*

(c) *Reserved.*

(d) *The member or transferee whose transferable interest is subject to a charging order under subsection (a) of this section may extinguish the charging order by satisfying the judgment and filing a certified copy of the satisfaction with the court that issued the charging order.*

(e) *A limited liability company or one (1) or more members whose transferable interests are not subject to the charging order may pay to the judgment creditor the full amount due under the judgment and thereby succeed to the rights of the judgment creditor, including the charging order.*

(f) *This article does not deprive any member or transferee of the benefit of any exemption laws applicable to the member's or transferee's transferable interest.*

(g) *This section provides the exclusive remedy by which a person seeking to enforce a judgment against a judgment debtor, including any judgment debtor who may be the sole member, dissociated member or transferee, may, in the capacity of the judgment creditor, satisfy the judgment from the judgment debtor's transferable interest or from the assets of the limited liability company. Other remedies, including foreclosure on the judgment debtor's limited liability interest and a court order for directions, accounts and inquiries that the judgment debtor might have made are not available to the judgment creditor attempting to satisfy a judgment out of the judgment debtor's interest in the limited liability company and may not be ordered by the court.*

Charging Order Protection
Wyoming

Limited Partnership
Wyoming Title 17
Chapter 14 - Limited Partnerships
Article 1 - Limited Partnership Act of 1971
Section 803 - Rights of Creditor
Section 804 - Right of Assignee to Become Limited Partner

803 On application to a court of competent jurisdiction by any judgment creditor of a partner, the court may charge the partnership interest of the partner with payment of the unsatisfied amount of the judgment with interest. To the extent so charged, the judgment creditor has only the rights of an assignee of the partnership interest. This act does not deprive any partner of the benefit of any exemption laws applicable to his partnership interest.

804 (a) An assignee of a partnership interest, including an assignee of a general partner, may become a limited partner if and to the extent that:
  (i) The assignor gives the assignee that right in accordance with authority described in the partnership agreement; or
  (ii) All other partners consent.

(b) An assignee who has become a limited partner has, to the extent assigned, the rights and powers, and is subject to the restrictions and liabilities, of a limited partner under the partnership agreement and this act. An assignee who becomes a limited partner also is liable for the obligations of his assignor to make and return contributions as provided in articles 6 and 7. However, the assignee is not obligated for liabilities unknown to the assignee at the time he became a limited partner.

(c) If an assignee of a partnership interest becomes a limited partner, the assignor is not released from his liability to the limited partnership under W.S. 17-14-307 and 17-14-602.

Internal Revenue Service
Revenue Ruling 1977-1 C.B. 178
Section 761 - Partnership Definitions

Headnote

Limited partnership; assignment of interest. An assignee acquiring substantially all of the dominion and control over the interest of a limited partner is treated as a substituted limited partner for Federal income tax purposes.

IRS Revenue Ruling 77-137

A, a limited partner in a limited partnership formed under the Uniform Limited Partnership Act of a state, assigned the limited partnership interest to B. The agreement of the partnership provides, in part, that assignees of limited partners may not become substituted limited partners in the partnership without the written consent of the general partners. However, it also provides that a limited partner may, without the consent of the general partners, assign irrevocably to another the right to share in the profits and losses of the partnership and to receive all distributions, including liquidating distributions, to which the limited partner would have been entitled had the assignment not been made. Under the terms of the assignment A, who was the nominal limited partner under local law, agreed to exercise any residual powers remaining in A solely in favor of and in the interest of B.

Held, even though the general partners did not give their consent to the assignment, since B, the assignee, acquired substantially all of the dominion and control over the limited partnership interest, for Federal income tax purposes B is treated as a substituted limited partner. Therefore, B must report the distributive share of partnership items of income, gain, loss, deduction, and credit attributable to the assigned interest on B's Federal income tax return in the same manner and in the same amounts that would be required if B was a substituted limited partner.

IRS Revenue Ruling 77-137

A judgement creditor is obligated under IRS Revenue Ruling 77-137 to report and pay taxes on their share of income regardless of whether such earnings are distributed or retained. Meaning, any monies allocated to a judgment creditor through a charging order would be treated as income and be subject to capital gains tax even if no actual money is received by the creditor. This allocation may not be accompanied with any money, thus causing "phantom income" to the creditor, whereby taxes are owed without money used to pay them. So even if a person wins a lawsuit against you they must still pay taxes on money they cannot collect! The most important components to the Charging Order protection are as follows:

Part 1   No Court will allow a creditor to reach into a Limited Liability Company, Limited Partnership or (Nevada) Corporation and take its safe assets to satisfy a personal judgment entered against you. By law an LLC, LP or Corp are legal third party persons, therefore the assets inside it are owned by the respective entity. Provided there were no fraudulent conveyances and the judgement was not related to an 'inside' lawsuit (discussed in the next chapter), the assets within the LLC, LP or Corp may not be attached in order to satisfy a judgment creditor.

Part 2   The Court may force you to hand over any profits you receive as a member, limited partner or shareholder, if any profits are in fact distributed. Should the court order a percentage of the distributed profits relinquished to a creditor, a member, partner or shareholder may (at his / her / its sole discretion) refuse to distribute any such profits. Monies can always be loaned to ultimate beneficial owners at reasonably low interest rates, if needed.

Part 3   Pursuant to Internal Revenue Service (IRS) Revised Ruling 77-137 any person who is legally entitled to receive profits from a Limited Liability Company, Limited Partnership or (Nevada) Corporation, the creditor may **not** seize any of the assets directly from the LLC, LP or Corp and may **not** collect on the distribution of profits if none are distributed. However such judgement creditors must still pay taxes on the profits even if no profits are distributed.

For what length of time do you believe a creditor would continue to pursue a judgement against a debtor when the creditor must continually pay taxes on money which they cannot collect? Is this not fair retribution for a frivolous law suit? As litigators say, *"They no longer want the cheese; they just want out of the trap!"*

Charging Order Protection
Analysis 1 of 4

Question

Will the courts interfere with an LLC or LP to satisfy a judgment against a member or partner?

Answer

Excluding a fraudulent transfer, the Uniform Partnership Act (1916) provides that a creditor of a partner cannot reach the assets of the partnership to satisfy the debt of that partner. Since it is the Limited Partnership (or LLC) and not the partner (or member) which owns the assets, the creditor has no claim against property that has been transferred to the LP.

Both an LLC member interests and an LP partner interests are subject to Charging Orders against the interest of the respective debtor member or partner. In California, prior to the adoption of the Uniform Partnership Act, a judgment creditor of a partner whose personal debt (as distinguished from partnership debt) gave rise to the judgment and could cause a sale of partnership assets including specific items of partnership property to satisfy his judgment. (Corporations Code 15001 et seq. generally stopped that ability)

In *Evans v. Galardi,*16 Cal.3d 300, the court refused to allow a levy on partnership assets to satisfy a partner's debt and the court required the creditor to use the Charging Order instead. Whereas in the instant case *Evans v. Galardi,*16 Cal.3d 300, the partnership is a viable business organization and plaintiff does not show that he will be unable to secure satisfaction of his judgment by use of a Charging Order or by levy of execution against the debtors' other personally owned property, there is no reason to permit deviation from the prescribed statutory process, (the Charging Order) *Crocker Nat. Bank v. Perroton*, 208 Cal. App. 3d 1(1989). In Nevada a Limited Partnership is protected from a partners judgment creditor:

Nevada Revised Statutes (NRS) 87.260
The property of a partnership belongs to the firm and not the partners

"A partner has no individual property in any specific assets of the firm. Instead, the interest of each partner in the partnership property is his share in the surplus, after the partnership debts are paid and the partnership accounts have been settled; until that time arrives, it cannot be known what property will have to be used to satisfy the debts and, and therefore, what property will remain after debts are paid." Nevada State v. Elsbury, 63 Nev. 463, 175 P.2d 430 (1946); Balaban v. Bank of Nev., 86 Nev. 862, 477 P.2d 860 (1970).

California Attitude

California's Corporate Code Section 16307(c) concludes that a judgment against a partnership is not itself a judgment against a partner. A judgment against a partnership may not be satisfied from a partners assets unless there is also a judgment against the partner.

By the same token a limited partner in an LP is further protected by NRS 88.535 (6), which states, *"No creditor of a partner has any right to obtain possession of, or otherwise exercise legal or equitable remedies with respect to, the property of the Limited Partnership."*

The same principle applies to a LLC in NRS 86.401, which states, *"No creditor of a member has any right to obtain possession of, or otherwise exercise legal or equitable remedies with respect to, the property of the Limited Liability Company."*

By statute and case law partner creditors may not touch any of the bank accounts or assets of a Limited Liability Company. In Colorado, as well as many other states like Nevada, California and Texas which have adopted the Uniform Partnership Act, partner assets remain protected. In *Watt, Tieder, Killian & Hoffar v. United States Fidelity & Guarantee*, 847 P.2d 170, the court states,

> *"Under the entity theory of partnership adopted in the Uniform Partnership Act, 7-60-101, et seq., C.R.S. (1986 Repl. Vol. 3A), partnership property is owned by the partnership entity, not the individual partners. Section 7-60-125, C.R.S. (1986 Repl. Vol. 3A). And, a partner's interest in the partnership is deemed personally and consists of a proportionate share of the firm's profits and surplus. Section 7-60-126, C.R.S. (1986 Repl. Vol. 3A). Hence, the trial court cannot order a division of specific partnership interest to a non-partner spouse if, as here, there are other partners in the venture besides the other spouse. Kalcevic v. Kalcevic, 156 Colo. 151, 397 P.2d 483 (1964); see generally 1-A. Bromberg & L. Ribstein, Bromberg & Ribstein on Partnership 3.05 (1988)."*

In California, *Crocker Nat. Bank v. Perroton*, 208 Cal. App. 3d 1(1989) states,

> *"A creditor with a judgment against a partner but not against the partnership ordinarily cannot execute directly on partnership assets or the partners interest in the partnership. (Advising California Partnerships 2d (Cont.Ed.Bar 1988) 6.88, p. 428, citing Code Civ. Proc., 699.720; see also Corp. Code, 15025, subd. (2) (c).) The reasons for the rule were discussed at some length in Taylor v. S & M Lamp Co.,190 Cal.App.2d 700, 707-708."*

Charging Order Protection
Analysis 2 of 4

Question

If a Charging Order is granted by the Court, can the judgment creditor try to collect by seizing Limited Liability Company or Limited Partnership assets on execution?

Answer

The theory behind a Charging Order concept is to prevent such seizure or disruption and allow the members or partners to continue to run the business of the respective LLC or LP undisturbed by any actions of a creditor against one member or partner. Nevada Revised Statute 87.280, which describes a partner's interest subject to Charging Order, provides that:

1. On due application to a competent court by any judgment creditor of a partner, the court which entered the judgment, order, or decree, or any other court, may charge the interest of the debtor partner with payment of the unsatisfied amount of such judgment debt with interest thereon; and may then or later appoint a receiver of his share of the profits, and of any other money due or to fall due to him in respect of the partnership, and make all other orders, directions, accounts and inquiries which the debtor partner might have made, or which the circumstances of the case may require.

2. The interest charged may be redeemed at any time before foreclosure, or in case of a sale being directed by the court may be purchased without thereby causing a dissolution:
   (a) With separate property, by any one or more of the partners; or
   (b) With partnership property, by any one or more of the partners with the consent of all the partners whose interests are not so charged or sold.

3. Nothing in this chapter shall be held to deprive a partner of his right, if any, under the exemption laws, as regards his interest in the partnership. §703 of the Revised Uniform Limited Partnership Act 1976 provides that on application to a court of competent jurisdiction by any judgment creditor of a partner, the court may charge the interest of the partner with payment of the unsatisfied amount of the judgment with interest. To the extent so charged, the judgment creditor has only the rights of an assignee of the partnership interest. This [Act] does not deprive any partner of the benefit of any exemption laws applicable to his or her partnership interest.

In effect, your creditor is only entitled to receive the income which you receive from the LLC or LP by virtue of your being a member or partner. Your creditor therefore has none of the rights that are even sparingly given to an LLC or LP and can do nothing but wait to receive whatever distributions (if any) may be made to you as a member or partner. Nevada has even stated that a judgment creditor does not have a right to request a pre-dissolution accounting of assets and income. *Bynum v. Frisby*, 311 P.2d 972 (1957). Your creditor, as an assignee, has no right to force you to make any distributions at all for the profits of the partnership. You also do not owe any duty of care to the assignee [your creditor] and can ignore his existence.

California Attitude

California has embodied the Revised Uniform Limited Partnership Act of 1976 into its Corporation Code. §15673 of the Corp Code provides that the judgment creditor has only the rights of an assignee of the limited partnership interest. §15674, provides that an assignee of a partnership interest, including an assignee of a general partner, may become a limited partner if and to the extent that the partnership agreement so provides or all partners consent. However, a California appeals court has ruled that the consent element is not rigid, and a court can order a judgment creditor to become a limited partner. *Hellman v. Anderson*, 233 Cal. App.3d 840, 284 Cal. Rptr. 830 (1991). The California appeals courts are split on the issue of partner consent. In the above case the third district recognized that another appeals court in California had held that consent of all partners was required. *Cocker National Bank v. Perroton*, 208 Cal. App.3d 1, 255 Cal Rptr. 794 (1989). The California Supreme Court has not taken up the issue as of yet so it remains to be seen as to how this conflict will be resolved. California, however, arguably should give deference to the partners if they can show that allowing a judgment creditor to become a limited partner would hamper the on going purpose of the partnership.

Cases supporting the proposition that a creditor can only charge the interest of the partner concerned, are the California Cases of:

Davidson v. Knox, (1885) 67c 143;
Sherwood v. Jackson, (1932) 121 C.A.354, 356;
Baum v. Baum, (1959) 51 C.2d 610, 613;
Ribero v. Callway, (1948) 87 C.A. 2d 135, 138; and
Citizens National Trust & Savings Bank v. McNeny, 10 CA2d 488.

The leading California case now is *Evans v. Galardi*, (1976) 1976 16 C3d 300 and (1979) 93 CA3d 291 in which it was held:

> *"A partner has no interest in the partnership property by virtue of his status as a limited partner, and as such assets are not available to satisfy judgment against the limited partner in his individual capacity....where the judgment creditor cannot secure satisfaction of his judgment by attaching personal property of the debtor, the court would make no exception to the general rule that a creditor has rights only to the income of the partnership [in which the debtor has a partnership interest]...."*

As an added discouragement for your creditor, the IRS takes the view that an assignee [your creditor] of a limited partnership interest who is not admitted as a partner will still be treated as a partner for federal tax purposes (Rev. Rule 77-137, 1977-1 C.A.178.). This means that your creditor as an assignee is taxed on your share of the profits of the Limited Partnership even if you did not receive any distribution of profits. So, while no profits were distributed to the creditor under the Charging Order your creditor pays federal taxes on monies he has not received (this is known as 'phantom income'). A case in support of the above IRS Ruling is *Jackson v. Commissioner*, (Para 81-954 PH Memo TC (1981)). This revenue ruling explains why a creditor only receives a Charging Order to the interest in a Limited Liability Company or Limited Partnership.

Charging Order Protection
Analysis 3 of 4

Question

What are the requirements that must be met for the foreclosure of a membership or partnership interest following a Charging Order?

Answer

There are only two basic requirements that must be met. First, there must be statutory authority for the foreclosure. Second, the owner of the interest must be on notice that the other party is seeking foreclosure. In only one case *Tupper v. Kroc*, 88 Nev. 146, 494 P.2d 1275 (1972), did the Nevada Supreme Court uphold a foreclosure of *Tupper's* partnership interest to satisfy the judgment creditor *Kroc*, but only when the creditor did not oppose it!

If a creditor succeeds with a sale made pursuant to a Charging Order of a partner's interest in a partnership it is not a sale of any assets in a partnership, only the partners share of ownership. A Charging Order cannot grant the creditor a greater interest in the partnership than that of the debtor partner at the time of the order. Not surprisingly, no case could be found regarding a foreclosure of a Limited Liability Company's interest.

Charging Order Protection
Analysis 4 of 4

Question

Can a judgment creditor order the court to issue a Writ of Garnishment on wages earned after the funds are in the hands of an employee?

Answer

Under Tex. Civ. Prac. & Rem. Code Section 63.004, Current wages for personal service are not subject to garnishment. Also Under Tex. Const. Art. XVI Section 28, No current wages for personal service shall ever be subject to garnishment, except for the enforcement of court ordered child support payments.

Notwithstanding the above, in the case entitled *American Express Travel Related Services v. Court of Appeals of Texas*, 14th Dist., Houston, 831 S.W. 2d 531 (Tx. App. 1992), the Texas Court of Appeals held that Texas courts have held that when wages are paid to and received by the wage-earner, they cease to be current for purposes of the exemption laws (citation omitted). In this case the Court reasoned that when appellee received his paychecks from his employer and deposited them into his checking account with garnishee bank, such wages were no longer exempt and where properly subject to garnishment by Appellant.

Following the case, *Davis v. Raborn*, 754 S.W. 2d 481 (Tx. Ct. App. 1988), which held that for the purposes of the above statutes, wages remain current and exempt until paid to and received by the wage earner. (Citations omitted). The court then stated, *"We therefore reject Appellants argument that his paychecks remain current wages until deposited and honored by his employers bank."* The case law is clear the wages lose their current status when the wage earner is paid by his employer. (Id at 483).

Asset Protection Services of America

Inside Lawsuit

Outside Lawsuit

Inside and Outside Lawsuits

AssetProtectionServices.com

Types of Assets

Low Risk   Assets of intrinsic value which are *not* subject to creating an inside lawsuit such as cash, stocks, bonds, mutual funds, CD's, gold, silver, coins, jewelry, or artwork, etc.

High Risk   Assets of intrinsic value which *may* cause an inside lawsuit such as your home, cars, boats, planes, rental properties or businesses, etc.

To protect yourself and your family, avoid making costly errors while assigning your valuable high-risk and low-risk assets. To do this effectively, you simply must understand the difference between an 'inside' and an 'outside' lawsuit and how that distinction affects the charging order protection.

Outside Lawsuits

If the ownership of a privately registered vehicle became involved in an accident wherein a lawsuit ensued, the "cause of action" for such lawsuit would be the automobile accident. Because the automobile accident would **not** have had a direct relationship with the business of the entity, such as a Limited Liability Company (LLC), Limited Partnership (LP) or (Nevada) Corporation (Corp), it would *not* be listed in the lawsuit. However, if the Plaintiff's attorney chose to pursue the assets of the entity it would be considered an "outside" lawsuit. This concept can be further understood by viewing the submarine above. Just like the torpedo is bouncing off the hull of the craft, so too would the Plaintiff hit the "Charging Order Protection" and be deflected from reaching any of the assets within the LLC, LP or (Nevada) Corp.

Inside Lawsuits

If the ownership of a rental home was titled into an LLC, LP or Corp along with an apartment building and beach house and the rental home caught fire, a lawsuit may well ensue. The "cause of action" for that lawsuit would be the rental home fire. Because the rental home fire *would* have been directly involved with the business of the entity, the LLC, LP or Corp *would* be listed in the lawsuit. If the Plaintiff's attorney chose to pursue the assets of the entity it would be considered an "inside" lawsuit. This concept can be further understood by viewing the submarine above. Do you see the dotted lines 'separating' one home from the other inside the craft? Many investors are mistaken in their belief that the "Charging Order Protection" offers universal protection when, in fact, it does not.

The Charging Order Protection does __NOT__ apply to an Inside Lawsuit!

Bad News   Once a lawsuit ensues and the cause of action is determined to be related directly to the business operations of an LLC, LP or Corp it is the equivalent of having the submarine punctured. Outside of encumbrances, equity stripping and insurance, there is little (if anything) which can protect the other assets owned within the business entity from being pursued by a Plaintiff's attorney and seized by a judgement creditor.

Good News   Members of an LLC, limited partners of a LP and shareholders of a (Nevada) Corporation are *not* liable for the debts and obligations of the entity. There is no personal liability for any member, limited partner or shareholder beyond the scope of their investment into the entity. Member, limited partner and shareholder losses are contained (isolated) to their respective capital or equity investment in the LLC, LP or Corp.

Compartmentalization

The destruction of the rental home due to fire was unfortunate and hopefully the insurance policy would compensate for such loss. However, the judgement creditor seizing all equity in the apartment building and beach house was unnecessary and avoidable. When an individual has valuable assets, they should be placed into separate entities based on the overall value and risk of the asset. This concept can be further understood by viewing the submarines above. Had the properties been compartmentalized and titled into separate entities the loss would have been isolated. Should assets contain enough equity, the costs to form and maintain bank accounts, bookkeeping and file annual tax returns for multiple entities is an easy, logical and tax-deductible decision.

Asset Protection Services of America

Piercing the Corporate Veil

AssetProtectionServices.com

Introduction

The subject matter of 'Piercing the Corporate Veil' is equally applicable to Limited Liability Companies and Limited Partnerships as it is to Corporations. Each state has a different series of tests which it applies to determine whether the courts can pierce the corporate veil to get to the assets of the entity.

Individual Liability Protection

Nevada has the strictest tests and affords the highest degree of protection from lawsuits filed by disgruntled creditors and overzealous plaintiffs attorneys of any state in America (followed by Wyoming). Nevada has developed a strong record of case law that protects the corporate veil, making it the most difficult to pierce of any state in the country.

It wasn't until the 1950's that Nevada's Supreme Court began to seriously consider setting aside the corporate veil as a means of compensating someone that had been damaged by the acts of a corporation's principals. *[Nevada Tax Commission v. Hicks, 73 Nev. 115, 310 P.2d 852 (2957)]*. Even so, Nevada courts have traditionally been unwilling to pierce the corporate veil except in those various instances in which a fraud has been perpetrated to the damage of another and circumstances are particularly egregious. In fact, since 1978 only one Nevada "C" corporation has had their corporate veil pierced *[Mosa v. Wilson-Bates Furniture Co., 94 Nev. 521, 583 P.2d 453 (1978)]* and that was in 1987 *[Polaris Industries Corp v. Kaplan, 103 Nev. 598, 747 P.3d 884 (1987)]*.

Simply put, the protection and anonymity for the officers, directors and stockholders of a Nevada Corporation are unparalleled with any other state in the union. The burden of proof rests entirely on the Plaintiff (the person filing the lawsuit) to prove *all three* of the following requirements in a court of law. Failure to prove any *one* of these three requirements will result in a failure to pierce the corporate veil and access to any the assets shall be denied. This is a nearly insurmountable task which most attorneys will not even attempt as the history of success in doing so is infinitesimal in Nevada.

Nevada Revised Statute (NRS) 78.747
Liability of stockholder, director or officer for debt or liability of corporation
(Added to NRS by 2001, 3170)

1. *Except as otherwise provided by specific statute, no stockholder, director or officer of a corporation is individually liable for a debt or liability of the corporation, unless the stockholder, director or officer acts as the alter ego of the corporation.*

2. *Stockholder, director or officer acts as the alter ego of a corporation if:*
   (a) *The corporation is influenced and governed by the stockholder, director or officer;*
   (b) *There is such unity of interest and ownership that the corporation and the stockholder, director or officer are inseparable from each other;*

    (c) *Adherence to the corporate fiction of a separate entity would sanction fraud or promote a manifest injustice.*

3.   *The question of whether a stockholder, director or officer acts as the alter ego of a corporation must be determined by the court as a matter of law.*

Analysis of NRS 78.747

1.) The corporation must be influenced and governed by the person asserted to be the alter ego. When a corporation is not operating as a true legal entity and is being used by its shareholders as a "shell" to control private interests and assets or debts, the corporation is said to be the "alter ego" of its shareholders. A corporation may appear to be the alter ego of its shareholders when:
- No directors are elected;
- No corporate records are kept;
- No records are maintained by the shareholders;
- Personal funds or assets of shareholders are co-mingled with those of the company; (e.g. no separate bank accounts).

If the shareholders have themselves disregarded the corporate form, the law will disregard the entity and shall not offer shareholders the protection normally granted to the corporation.

2.) There must be such unity of interest and ownership that one is inseparable from the other;

3.) The facts must be such that adherence to the corporate fiction of a separate entity would, under the circumstances, sanction fraud or promote injustice.

Again, if any of these points are not successfully proven the action fails. The landmark case on this issue is the Nevada case *[Roland vs. Lepire, 99 Nev. 308, 662 P 2d. 1332 (1983)]*. In this case it was clear that the corporation was under capitalized, having a negative net worth at the time of the trial, there were no directors formalized, shareholders meetings were never held, there were no dividends were elected to paid to shareholders, no officers or directors ever received salaries (salaries and bonuses can be 'forgotten' if the company is not profitable) , there was no corporate minute book and no evidence that any minutes were kept. The corporation did obtain a general contractors license and framing contractor's license in its name, but that was the only evidence in support of the idea that it was a corporation.

The court concluded, *"Although the evidence does show that the corporation was undercapitalized and that there was little existence separate and apart from the two shareholders, the evidence was insufficient to support a finding that appellants were the alter ego of the corporation."* Thus the Nevada Supreme Court made it clear that unless the plaintiff is able to meet the burden of proving 'the financial setup of the corporation is a sham and caused an injustice' the veil is highly unlikely to be pierced.

Nevada Entities Sued by Another State

What happens when a Nevada corporation is sued under the jurisdiction and/or laws of another state? The lawsuit protection features of a corporation are available only if the integrity of the corporation as a separate or distinct entity (apart from the individual) is respected by the court and state taxing authorities.

In matters involving a lawsuit by an injured party, especially if a corporation has no significant assets, the plaintiff will attempt to convince the court that the corporate entity should not be respected and that the principals of the company should be personally liable.

There are many reported cases on this topic and the outcome is usually determined by whether the corporation carries out its business and if the corporation looks and acts the way a corporation should. If the principals treat the corporation and hold out the corporation to third parties as a separate and distinct entity, the court will usually uphold the status of the corporation and will not establish personal liability. However, if required corporate formalities are not consistently observed, the corporation may be disregarded and the individuals could be held personally liable.

Corporate Formalities

The following corporate formalities are those which, in general, the courts in most states have determined to be of particular significance:

Corporate Bylaws

The corporation must adopt a set of bylaws which provide a written statement of how the internal affairs of the corporation shall be handled. The bylaws set the time and place of regular shareholder meetings and meetings of the board of directors.

Corporate Minute Book

The corporate minute book contains a written record of actions by the shareholders and directors of the corporation. At a minimum, there must be annual minutes reflecting the election of directors by the shareholders. Any significant corporate activities, including corporate borrowings and major purchases should be properly reflected in the minutes of the meetings of the directors and shareholders.

Corporate Stock Ledger Book

If a Corporation issues any stock, the corporation must maintain an accurate stock ledger book. The stock ledger book shows who has been issued stock certificates and the amounts received by the corporation for the issuance of its stock. The stock ledger book also contains up-to-date records of the names and number of shares owned by each shareholder.

✓ Conducting Business in the Corporate Name

When doing business with third parties, the officers and directors must make it clear that they are acting on behalf of the corporation and not in their individual capacity. Correspondence should be sent out under the proper corporate letterhead and contracts should be entered into only in the name of the corporate authorized signatory. Unless documents clearly reflect that a transaction is entered into on behalf of the corporation, and all necessary agreements are entered into under the corporation, the corporate entity will not survive a challenge in a lawsuit.

✓ Corporate Bank Account

Corporate bank accounts and accounting records must be separate and distinct from the individual. A corporate bank account cannot be treated as if it were the account of an individual officer or director. Corporate income and assets must be separately accounted for on the books of the corporation. One of the biggest mistakes made by people is that they feel free to move money and property back and forth between themselves and their corporation without properly accounting for such movement in the records of the corporation. This is a fatal mistake, and under these circumstances, the court will disregard the corporate entity.

✓ Bona Fide Corporate Presence

It is possible to have your case decided under Nevada law even though events transpired in another state if Nevada has a "substantial relationship to the parties" and it was so agreed in the disputed contract.

✓ *Contractual Choice of Law Provisions (General Rule)*

The policy behind recognizing the choice by the parties to a contract, of the law, which pertains to the contract, was well stated half a century ago by Max Rheinstein:

> *"If we regard it as one of the principal purposes of the conflict of laws to protect the justified expectations of the parties, then the intention of the parties rule is the one which fulfills that purpose better than any rival rule, and quite particularly better than the place of contracting rule. If the parties have agreed upon the application of some particular law, then they have thought and acted in accordance with it."*
> – Max Rheinstein (Essays on the Conflict of Laws)

Through the years many courts have followed this principle. For example, in *[A.S. Rampell, Inc. v. Hyster Co., 3 N.Y.2d 369, 144 N.E.2d 371, 165 N.Y.S.2d 475 (1957)]*, the issue was whether an oral modification of the written contract at issue was valid. Hyster Co. was an Oregon corporation doing business in New York. And under New York law the oral modification of the written contract would *not* be valid, however under Oregon it *would* be valid. The written contract with Rampell declared that Oregon law would control the agreement. Since Oregon had a reasonable relationship to the choice-of-law of the parties, the New York court applied Oregon law and upheld the oral modification.

This rule applies even if the choice-of-law provision invalidates all or part of the contract. This is shown by *[Foreman v. George Foreman Assocs., Ltd. 517 F.2d 354 (9th Cir. 1975)]*. Here, boxer George Foreman, a California resident, entered into a boxing management contract with a Pennsylvania limited partnership. The contract stipulated that California law would apply. Foreman brought suit to avoid enforcement of the contract. The trial court found that since Foreman was a resident of California and the contract was signed there, the parties' choice-of-law was entitled to respect. Furthermore, since the contract violated several regulations promulgated by the California State Athletic Commission, the contract was invalid. The 9th Circuit Court of Appeals affirmed this ruling, on the ground that California has a strong public policy in protecting boxers from mortgaging their futures. If the choice-of-law provision was not enforced; the public policy would be violated. (Id. at 356-57). The rules revealed by these and other cases have found their way into:

Restatement of Conflict of Laws
(Second) Section 187(I)

(1) *The law of the state chosen by the parties to govern their contractual rights and duties will be applied if the particular issue is one which the parties could have resolved by an explicit provision in their agreement directed to that issue.*

"The Restatement recognizes [that] there should be no limitation on the power of the parties to incorporate foreign law into their contract." – Robert Allen Sedler

Source: The Contracts Provisions of the Restatement (Second): An Analysis and A Critique, 72 Colum. L. Rev. 279, 287 (1972)

Continuing on the same line of reason, under Section 187(2), the express choice-of-law is still recognized:

Restatement of Conflict of Laws
(Second) Section 187(2)

Even if the particular issue is one, which the parties could not have resolved, by an explicit provision in their agreement directed to that issue.

There are, however, three exceptions to Section 187(2).

First   *The chosen state has no substantial relationship to the parties or the transaction and there is no other reasonable basis for the parties' choice.*

Second   *Misrepresentation, duress, undue influence, or mistake secured the consent of one of the parties to the inclusion of the provision.*

Third   *Application of the state's law chosen would be contrary to a fundamental policy of the state that would be able to apply its own law but for the choice-of-law provision.*

– Sedler, supra, 72 Colum. L. Rev. at 290

In addition to the Restatement, under Section 1-105 of the Uniform Commercial Code (UCC), which is recognized in all 50 states, allows parties entering into a commercial contract to choose the applicable state law, so long as the transaction, *"Bears a reasonable relation to the state chosen."*

Thus, the general law of this country is that parties to a contract may choose the law of a state to govern the contract and that courts will uphold their choice in order to further the expectations of the parties.

Legal Entities

The government and most courts generally apply a five-point test to decide if a corporation is truly a properly run corporation and therefore a 'legal entity'. Such tests include:

✓ **Does the corporation have a physical presence in the state of incorporation?**
A Resident Agent / Registered Office address is *not* a physical presence in the state, as far as meeting this test is concerned, unless that same address is also providing your company's headquarters address with 'business address' and 'mail-forwarding' services as well.

✓ **Does the corporation have a telephone number that is answered in the name of the corporation in the state of incorporation?**
In today's era of technology, it is possible to order online numbers (through Skype for example) which can offer 'state specific' telephone numbers that ring-through to your computer or even forward to your cell phone.

✓ **Does the corporation have a bank account in the state of incorporation?**
Although a bank account can be set up in any state, Nevada entities should have a corporate bank account which 'originated' in Nevada.

✓ **Does the corporation conduct business in the name of the corporation or that of an officer, director or shareholder?**
The name, address and contact information of the corporation should appear on all invoices, contracts, business cards, websites, advertising, etc.

✓ **Does the corporation have any type of licenses in the state of incorporation?**
Although the $200 annual business licensing fee in the state of Nevada may have its (financial) draw-backs, it adds a layer of credibility by documenting the legality of the entity.

While there are several other factors to be considered by the government and the courts, these are the primary factors at least initially scrutinized.

Choice of Law

If an entity was incorporated in Nevada and is later 'foreign filed' in another state, which means it is 'registered as conducting business' in another state (i.e. California), then these tests shall apply to the 'home state' of incorporation (Nevada) as well. Even though an entity may be foreign-filed (i.e. in California), in the 'home state' of incorporation (Nevada) the laws and rules of the incorporating state (Nevada) shall apply to that corporation so long as the contract expressly claims Nevada as the venue in the agreement.

Benefits to Choice of Law Clauses

To highlight the benefit of incorporating in Nevada, and thus having a reasonable basis for choosing Nevada in a choice-of-law clause, it is necessary to review what can occur in the absence of such clauses. As an example, should a Nevada Corporation do business in California and be sued in the California courts for actions arising out of the business conducted in that state, the California courts would apply a three-part test to determine which state laws would apply to the case:

First   A determination is reached as to whether the two concerned states have differing laws;

Second   It considered whether each state has an interest in having its respective law applied to the case; and

Third   If the laws are different, and each state has an interest in having its own law applied, they apply the law of the state whose *"Interests would be more impaired if its policy were subordinated to the policy of the other state."*
[Havlicek v. Coast-To Coast Analytical Services, Inc., 39 Cal. App.4th 1844, 1851, 46 Cal. Rptr.2d 696, 699 (1995)] and *[North American Asbestos Corp. v. Superior Court, 180 Cal. App.3d 902, 905, 225 Cal. Rptr. 877, 879 (1986)].*

If a person incorporates in Nevada (or another state) and conducts business in California, the courts in California will generally apply its own laws to an action involving that corporation. However, with the use of forum-selection, venue-selection or choice-of-law clauses, this can be avoided. And, if the incorporation occurred in Nevada (as opposed to another state), the contract or agreement can stipulate the use of Nevada law and Nevada courts thus affording protection for the personal assets of the corporation's owners, as Nevada courts are far less likely to 'pierce the corporate veil' than California courts.

Moreover, in an attempt to "seize" jurisdiction, states (especially California) will attempt to demonstrate the majority of the corporation's business is being conducted in their state. One means to demonstrate in which state a corporation is conducting business is by reviewing the corporate bank deposits. If a Nevada Corporation deposits the vast majority of its funds in a bank in your home state (like California) instead of in Nevada, your home state may have no trouble showing that your business is being conducted in California instead of Nevada. Therefore, your home state will have a good chance of seizing jurisdiction and you may loose all safe guards available to a Nevada Corporations placing **_all_** your personal assets at risk.

Forum Selection Clauses

The approval of 'forum selection' clauses came in the court case of *[Smith, Valentino & Smith, Inc. v. Superior Court, 17 Cal.3d 491, 551P.2d 1206, 131 Cal. Rptr. 374 (1976)]*. Here, a Pennsylvania corporation entered into a contract with a California corporation. The contract included a reciprocal forum selection clause, wherein if the Pennsylvania Corporation brought suit it had to do so in Los Angeles, while the California Corporation could only sue on the contract in Philadelphia. The contract also stipulated that, wherever a suit was brought, Pennsylvania law would govern. The California Corporation brought suit in California alleging breach of contract and other issues. The trial court refused to hear the suit, pointing to the forum selection clause.

The California Supreme Court affirmed stating *"choice-of-law provisions are usually respected by California courts."* Id. at 494, 131 Cal. Rptr. at 376. The court also stated that, although there is a public policy favoring access to California courts by resident plaintiffs:

"(We) likewise conclude that the policy is satisfied in those cases where, as here, a plaintiff has freely and voluntarily negotiated away his right to a California forum. In so holding we are in accord with the modern trend, which favors enforceability of such forum selection clauses."

-   California Supreme Court
-

Nevada Venue

By incorporating in the state of Nevada, Nevada can by selected as the venue (choice-of-law and forum-selection) for contractual provisions. Remember, a primary purpose for incorporating in Nevada is to protect personal assets from the reach of creditors. So, if a Nevada court hears a case involving a Nevada corporation, using Nevada law, the chances of 'piercing the corporate veil' occurring are slim-to-none especially over issues such as under capitalization. Lastly, if a person were domiciled in Nevada and should their corporate veil ever be pierced the exemption laws available in Nevada allow for substantial protection of assets, and these can be also used in a bankruptcy proceeding.

Corporations

AssetProtectionServices.com

Nevada and Wyoming Corporations

Nevada Company Law	Nevada Revised Statute - Chapter 78
Wyoming Company Law	Wyoming Title 17 - Chapter 16
Official Document Language	English
Conduct Business Internationally	Yes
Conduct Business in United States	Yes
Resident Agent Required	Yes
Registered Office Required	Yes
Resident Secretary Required	No
Company Taxation	0 % State Income Tax *(Liable Federal Tax)*
Double Taxation Avoidance Agreements	No
Tax Resident Qualification	No
Income Tax	No State Income Tax *(Corp or Individual)*
Business Tax	Yes
Detailed Client Application Required	No
Minimum Shareholders	1 *(2 for Nevada Charging Order Protection)* *(0 for All 'Non-Profit' Corporations)*
Entity Shareholders Allowed	Yes
Residency of Shareholders Allowed	Any Nationality
Register of Shareholders	No
Register of Shareholders Public Record	No
Bearer Shares Permitted	No
Minimum Directors	1
Entity Directors Allowed	No
Residency of Directors Allowed	Any Nationality
Register of Directors	Yes *(Secretary of State)*
Register of Directors Public Record	Yes *(Nominee Directors Permitted)*
Disclosure of Shareholders to Reg. Agent	Yes
Disclosure of Shareholders with SOS	No
Annual General Meeting Required	No
Shareholders / Directors Meeting Required	Yes *(Anywhere in the World or by Proxy)*
Corporation Minutes and Resolutions	In Private Possession of Shareholder(s)
Corporation Seal Required	No *(But Highly Recommended)*
Minimum Paid Up Capital Required	No
Maximum Authorized Capital Investment	Unlimited
Capital Considerations	Any Currency or in Kind
Subject to Currency Controls & Restrictions	No
Application Fees	No

	Wyoming	Nevada
Annual Government Fees	$100 First Year	$450 to $750 First Year
	$50 Thereafter	$350 to $650 Thereafter

Keeping of Accounts Required	Yes
Filing of Accounts and Returns Required	Yes
Annual Government Return Filing Fees	No
Auditing of Accounts Required	No
Re-Domicile from a Foreign State	Yes
Re-Domicile to a Foreign State	Yes
Shelf Companies Available	No

	Wyoming	Nevada
Incorporation Time	3-5 Business Days	24 Hours *($125 Fee)*

Corporation (Corp)

A Corporation is a "person" and has a separate legal personality which can own and operate businesses, hire employees, buy and sell real estate, provide goods and services, rent office spaces, make contracts, have bank accounts, maintain retirement plans for employees, and sue and be sued. The existence of a Corporation is not affected by the death or bankruptcy of a shareholder, officer or director, but has a continuous existence as long as it complies with the statutory requirements of the state wherein it was incorporated. The corporate board of directors may elect to have the fiscal year-end coincide with the calendar year-end, a fiscal quarter, or any calendar month of its choosing. "C" Corporations file an 1120 tax election with the Internal Revenue Service (IRS) and file a separate annual tax return from those of an 'S' Corporation which files an 1120-S, or an individual who files a 1040. Double taxation can occur upon the distribution of dividends to corporations whose shareholders are also employees. Profits may be kept as retained earnings and taxed at the corporate level or properly reinvested for further growth. The great state of Nevada is the only state in the union which, in addition to having no formal personal income tax or corporate income tax, has extended the charging order protection to qualifying "C" Corporations.

'Shareholders'

Owners of Corporations are known as 'shareholders' and can posses varying degrees of voting rights and preferences to company assets. Nevada and Wyoming shareholders include, but are not limited to:

1.) Bearer *(Wyoming)*	**3.)** No Par Value	**5.)** Preferred	**7.)** Voting
2.) Common	**4.)** Non-Voting	**6.)** Redeemable	

Types of Corporations

'Alien'

An 'Alien' corporation operates in one or more countries outside the one in which it was formed . (A corporation is formed in Nevada and conducts business in Canada.)

'C'

When a corporation is created with the Secretary of State, they are all initially created as "C" corporations filing an 1120 tax return. However once the entity is formed a different tax election may be made, such as an 'S' or '501(c)(3)' tax election. "C" corporations are 'artificial persons' and obtain Employer Identification Numbers (EIN) whereas 'individuals' obtain a Social Security Number (SSN). "C" Corporations allow for an unlimited number of stockholders and their corporate assets, debts and taxes are separate from its shareholders.

'Closely Held'

A 'Closely Held' corporation is where a family or close group of people own its shares and are usually not sold outside the family or group. One method of determining if a corporation is closely held is to check and see if at any time during the previous six months more than 50% of the value of its outstanding stock are owned directly or indirectly by five or fewer individual.

'Domestic'

A 'Domestic' corporation operates in the state in which it was formed. (A corporation is formed in Nevada and conducts business in Nevada.)

'Foreign'

A 'Foreign' corporation operates in one or more states outside the one in which it was formed. (A corporation is formed in Nevada and conducts business in California.)

'Holding'

When one corporation controls another corporation, usually called subsidiaries, then it is considered a 'Holding' corporation. A holding corporation maintains control of its subsidiary when it owns at least 80% of its stock. The IRS will allow, but may request, a holding corporation to combine their income and expenses and file a consolidated tax return that includes all subsidiaries.

'Personal Holding'

The IRS designates any corporation with over 60% of its income being passive, and for which five or less people own over 50% of the stock at any time during the last 6 months of the tax year, to be a 'Personal Holding' corporation. Under the stock ownership principle, the rules consider stock owned by a corporation, partnership, or estate to be owned proportionately by its shareholders, partners, or beneficiaries.

'Personal Service'

A 'Personal Service' corporation is determined by function and ownership and is generally operated by lawyers, accountants, consultants, architects, engineers and psychiatrists, etc. We rarely recommend this entity as there is a 35% flat tax on all personal service corporations. There are other more suitable choices available such as professional corporations and professional limited liability companies.

'Professional'

A 'Professional' corporation or "PC" (some states refer to them as a 'Professional Association' or "PA") is a sub-category of a personal service corporation. The primary distinction is that the owner must be licensed or otherwise legally authorized to render professional services. In most instances, a professional corporation or association may only offer one type of professional service at a time and is prohibited from simultaneously conducting any other types of business or service.

'Public' vs. 'Private'

A 'Public' corporation, such as Microsoft or General Electric, is one which is registered with the Securities Exchange Commission (SEC) and has stock available for purchase on the open market with a stock exchange such as the New York Stock Exchange (NYSE). A 'Private' corporation is one in which the stock of the company is not available for sale on any public market.

'S'

An "S" corporation is a "C" corporation which has made an "S" tax election by filing IRS Form 2553. This change allows the corporation to be taxed like a sole proprietorship or partnership instead of a separate entity. The primary difference is earnings or profits pass through directly to the shareholder's personal 1040 tax return. "S" corporations typically match their fiscal year-end with the calendar year-end and all profits are taxed evenly, if not distributed. State taxes apply to individuals who reside in certain states such as California (even thought the business may not be operating in the state) with an individual state income tax. "S" corporations may have a maximum of 100 shareholders with one class of stock and are generally smaller sized companies. "S" corporations file an 1120-S tax return with the IRS.

'Sole'

A non-profit corporation specifically designated for religious endeavors is a corporation 'Sole'. It can be formed to acquire, hold or dispose of church or religious society property for the benefit of religion, works of charity or public worship.

'Non Profit'

A 'Non Profit' corporation is formed at the state level and is considered a 'for profit' business at the federal level by the IRS for tax purposes. Non profit corporations file an 1120 tax election with the IRS, just like all "C" Corporations do, regardless of the state of formation. However, unlike 'for profit' corporations, 'non profit' corporations may *not* issue stock and are generally not subject to paying for any state business licensing fees.

A non profit corporation is *not* a IRS 501 (c) tax-exempt entity upon formation. Meaning, creating a non profit organization at the state level does not grant the organization exemption from paying corporate income tax at the federal level. The 501 (c) tax exempt status can only be acquired by applying to the IRS and requesting the tax exemption after a state non-profit corporation has been formed. The 501 (c) federal tax exemption is then only recognized if the IRS approves the application and grants the 'non profit' corporation the status of 'tax exempt'.

'501(c)(3)'

501(c)(3) organizations are a type of non-profit corporation which have filed for tax-exemption at the federal level and are classified by the IRS as a "public charity" or "private foundation." Within those two broad categories, a 501(c)(3) is further designated under one or more of the following categories; Charitable, Educational, Fostering National or International Amateur Sports Competitions, Literary, Promoting the Prevention of Cruelty to Children or Animals, Religious, Scientific, or Testing for Public Safety. Non-profit corporations which choose to file a

501(c)(3) with the IRS must have at least 5 directors or trustees and, upon dissolution, are required to distribute their assets to the state, the federal government or another entity.

Non Profit vs. Tax Exempt

A non profit entity is a state law concept. Although federal tax-exempt organizations begin as non-profit entities, creating a non-profit organization at the state level does **not** automatically grant the organization exemption from paying federal income tax. An entity is first formed as a non-profit at the state level (subject to federal income taxes) and may then choose to file for a tax-exempt status at the federal level; the two matters are not one-in-the-same.

For Profit vs. Non Profit (at State Level)

What distinguishes 'for-profit' and 'non profit' corporations is what can be *done* with any 'profit' created from the activities of the corporation. For-profit corporations generate net revenue and distribute those profits to their shareholders through dividends. A shareholder or individual is defined as a person having a personal ownership interest in the activities of the corporation. Non-profit corporations reduce their taxable net income by paying 'normal and necessary' operating expenses, just as 'for profit' corporations do, but are prohibited from distributing their profits to shareholders (because they have issued no stock and therefore no shareholders). It is this distinction, and not the ability to generate profit, which is the major difference between 'for profit' and 'non profit' corporations. Otherwise the two types of corporations enjoy the same form and function in every way, including operating their businesses to be as 'profitable' as they can be.

	For Profit	**Non Profit**
Income Tax	Corporations files form 1120 and pay income tax on net profit; Employees file Form 1040 and pay income tax on salaries received.	Non profits file Form 990 or 990-EZ and pay income tax only on net profits from unrelated activities; employees of the non-profit file Form 1040 and pay income tax on salaries received.
Payroll Taxes	Sole Proprietorships and Corporations file quarterly 941's and annual 940, W-2's and W-3.	Non-profits file quarterly 941's and annual W-2's/W-3. 501(c)(3) organizations do not pay FUTA tax (Form 940).
Charitable Contributions	Grantors and Contributors are not able to take a charitable contribution deduction for cash or goods donated to Individuals or to a for-profit organization,	Grantors and Contributors are permitted to take a charitable contribution deduction for cash or goods donated to a 501(c)(3) organization.

Non Profit 501(c) Companies

Non profit companies must not be organized or operated for the benefit of private interests, such as the creator or the creator's family, shareholders of the organization, or other designated individuals and persons controlled directly or indirectly by such private interests. No part of the net earnings of an IRC Section 501(c)(3) organization may inure to the benefit of any person. If the organization engages in an excess benefit transaction with a person having substantial influence over the organization, an excise tax may be imposed on the person and any managers agreeing to the transaction.

As a result of its qualification as a 501(c)(3) organization, such companies are able to receive tax-deductible charitable contributions and are exempt from business income and property taxes. However IRC section 501(c)(3) organizations are restricted in the amount of political and legislative (lobbying) activities they may conduct.

For an entity to qualify as tax-exempt from federal income taxes, the organization must meet requirements set forth in the Internal Revenue Code. Here is a brief list of the most common types of tax-exempt organizations as found in IRS Publication 557.

501(c) Classifications

501(c)(4) – Civic Leagues and Social Welfare Organizations

501(c)(5) – Labor, Agricultural, and Horticultural Organizations

501(c)(6 and 7) – Business Leagues, Chambers of Commerce, Social and Recreation Clubs

501(c)(8 and 10) – Fraternal Beneficiary Societies and Domestic Fraternal Societies

501(c)(4, 9 and 17) – Employees' Associations

501(c)(12) – Benevolent Life Insurance Associations, Mutual Irrigation, Telephone Companies

501(c)(13) – Cemetery Companies

501(c)(14) – Credit Unions and Other Mutual Financial Organizations

501(c)(19) – Veterans' Organizations

501(c)(20) – Group Legal Services Plan Organizations

501(c)(21) – Black Lung Benefit Trusts

501(c)(24) – Title-Holding Corporations for Single Parents

501(c)(25) – Title-Holding Corporations for Multiple Parents

501(c)(26) – State-Sponsored Health Coverage

501(c)(27) – Workman's Compensation Organizations

Charitable Entities

The term charitable, as used in its generally accepted legal sense, includes:
- Advancement of religion, education or science;
- Combating community deterioration and juvenile delinquency;
- Defense of human and civil rights secured by law;
- Elimination of prejudice and discrimination;
- Erection or maintenance of public buildings, monuments, or works;
- Lessening the burdens of government or neighborhood tensions;
- Relief to the poor, distressed or underprivileged.

Revised Uniform Model Business Corporation Act

Most states base their corporate law on the Revised Uniform Model Business Corporation Act as developed by the Committee on corporate Laws of the American Bar Association (ABA). For this reason, it should not be surprising to find similarities in the Corporation Codes of various states. However, the Model Act has been refined and modified over time and, because of the independence of the various states do not to conform entirely to the Model Act, each state has developed its own eccentricities that set it apart from the other states.

Under the Uniform Model Act, for instance, a stock certificate is required to contain:

1. the name of the issuing corporation and the state under which it is organized;
2. the name of the person to whom the stock is issued; and
3. the number and class of shares and the designation of the series (if any) that the certificate represents.

In the State of Nevada, one area which separates the Corporation Code from the Model Act is the information required on the stock certificate of a Corporation. Generally, the stock certificate is what evidences ownership of a corporation. However the Nevada Revised Statutes (NRS) reads differently. NRS 78.235(1) reads, in part, as follows:

"Every stockholder is entitled to have a certificate, signed by officers or agents designated by the corporation for the purpose, certifying the number of shares owned by him in the corporation."

In other words, Nevada law only requires two things on a corporate stock certificate:
1. the name of the corporation, and
2. the number of shares represented by the certificate.

Nevada Revised Statute (78.240) furthers shares of Nevada stock are **personal property**. So, all rules, regulations, and applicable taxes that would otherwise apply to transfers of personal property also apply to transfers of corporate stock.

Additionally, Nevada Revised Statutes states that a Nevada stock certificate is not stock in and of itself. Meaning the stockholder may own the stock with or without the stock certificate. The Nevada Attorney General published a formal opinion on this subject (AGO38). In that opinion he stated that:

"The certificate is merely a piece of paper that indicates ownership. Because Nevada does not require corporations to issue certificates at all, it would be foolish to assume that possession of the certificate equals ownership of the shares".

Nevada Privacy

There are only two tangible sources of information on relating to the ownership of a Nevada Corporation: the stock certificate (which are not required to be issued at all in Nevada), and the stock ledger. The stock ledger has its own legal requirements under Nevada law. The ledger must contain, in alphabetical order, the names of the stockholders, their residence address, and the number of shares owned by each.

This list must be revised annually, and would be a significant document for a legal adversary to obtain. However, Nevada law provides a statutory barrier to getting and using information on the stock ledger. NRS 78.257 provides that any stockholder who owns at least 15% of the issued shares of a corporation has a right to inspect the corporate books and records upon five days notice. But subsection 3 of that statute states,

"Any stockholder or other person exercising (these rights) who uses or attempts to use information, documents, records or other data obtained from the corporation or LLC, for any purpose not related to the stockholder's/members interest in the corporation/LLC as a stockholder/member, would be guilty of a gross misdemeanor".

In other words, the penalty for using corporate/membership information for any other purpose than to have a stockholder/member defend or demonstrate his/her interest in the corporation/ LLC is punishable up to one year in jail and up to a $2,000 fine. Clearly, a non-stockholder/ member in a Nevada Corporation or LLC has no legal right or authority whatsoever to view the stock or membership ledger. However, a court order from a court of competent jurisdiction would be enough to establish a reasonable cause to view the ledgers.

Nevada Transfer of Ownership

Most of the confusion surrounding corporate shares and/or membership interest has to deal with the issue of transferring ownership. If a stock or membership certificate is made transferable to the order of 'John Doe', it is negotiated by delivery with an endorsement (signature and proof of identity). Nevada case law requires a transfer of stock to be registered upon the corporation's books before the transfer is valid against the corporation. This is done to protect corporate officers in determining ownership of and the right to vote their shares. *[61 Nev. 431, 132 P.2d 605 (1942)]*

Individual Liability Protection

Nevada
Corporation

A Nevada Corporation may even indemnify officers and directors whether an action be civil, criminal, administrative or investigative if they are a director, officer, employee or agent (etc) against expenses, including attorney's fees, judgments, fines and amounts paid in a settlement.

Nevada Revised Statute (NRS) 78.7502
Discretionary and mandatory indemnification of
officers, directors, employees and agents: General provisions
(Added to NRS by 1997, 694; A 2001, 3175)

1. A corporation may indemnify any person who was or is a party or is threatened to be made a party to any threatened, pending or completed action, suit or proceeding, whether civil, criminal, administrative or investigative, except an action by or in the right of the corporation, by reason of the fact that the person is or was a director, officer, employee or agent of the corporation, or is or was serving at the request of the corporation as a director, officer, employee or agent of another corporation, partnership, joint venture, trust or other enterprise, against expenses, including attorneys' fees, judgments, fines and amounts paid in settlement actually and reasonably incurred by the person in connection with the action, suit or proceeding if the person:
(a) Is not liable pursuant to NRS 78.138; or
(b) Acted in good faith and in a manner which he or she reasonably believed to be in or not opposed to the best interests of the corporation, and, with respect to any criminal action or proceeding, had no reasonable cause to believe the conduct was unlawful. The termination of any action, suit or proceeding by judgment, order, settlement, conviction or upon a plea of nolo contendere or its equivalent, does not, of itself, create a presumption that the person is liable pursuant to NRS 78.138 or did not act in good faith and in a manner which he or she reasonably believed to be in or not opposed to the best interests of the corporation, or that, with respect to any criminal action or proceeding, he or she had reasonable cause to believe that the conduct was unlawful.

3. To the extent that a director, officer, employee or agent of a corporation has been successful on the merits or otherwise in defense of any action, suit or proceeding referred to in subsections 1 and 2, or in defense of any claim, issue or matter therein, the corporation shall indemnify him or her against expenses, including attorneys' fees, actually and reasonably incurred by him or her in connection with the defense.

Individual Liability Protection

Wyoming
Corporation

Wyoming Title 17
Chapter 16
Section 622 - Liability of Shareholders

(a) A purchaser from a corporation of its own shares is not liable to the corporation or its creditors with respect to the shares except to pay the consideration for which the shares were authorized to be issued pursuant to W.S. 17-16-621 or specified in the subscription agreement pursuant to W.S. 17-16-620.

(b) Unless otherwise provided in the articles of incorporation, a shareholder of a corporation is not personally liable for the acts or debts of the corporation except that he may become personally liable by reason of his own acts or conduct.

Wyoming Title 17
Chapter 16
Section 842 - Standards of Conduct for Officers

(d) An officer shall not be liable to the corporation or its shareholders for any decisions to take or not to take action as an officer, or any failure to take any action, if he performed the duties of his office in compliance with this section. Whether an officer who does not comply with this section shall have liability shall depend in such instance on applicable law, including those principles of W.S. 17-16-831 that have relevance.

Limited Liability Companies

Nevada and Wyoming   Limited Liability Companies

Nevada Company Law	Nevada Revised Statute - Chapter 86
Wyoming Company Law	Wyoming Title 17 - Chapter 29
Official Document Language	English
Conduct Business Internationally	Yes
Conduct Business in United States	Yes
Conduct Business in State	Yes
Resident Agent Required	Yes
Registered Office Required	Yes
Resident Secretary Required	No
Company Taxation	0 % State Income Tax *(Liable Federal Tax)*
Double Taxation Avoidance Agreements	No
Tax Resident Qualification	No
Income Tax	No State Income Tax *(Corp or Individual)*
Business Tax	No
Detailed Client Application Required	No
Minimum Members	1 *(Single-Member)*, 2 *(Multi-Member)*
Entity Members Allowed	Yes
Residency of Members Allowed	Any Nationality
Register of Members	Yes *(Secretary of State)*
Register of Members Public Record	Yes *(But Only the Managing Member)*
Disclosure of Members to Registered Agent	Yes
Disclosure of Members with SOS	Yes *(Nevada)*
Annual General Meeting Required	No
Members Meeting Required	Yes *(Anywhere in the World or by Proxy)*
Company Resolutions	In Private Possession of Member(s)
Company Seal Required	No *(But Highly Recommended)*
Minimum Paid Up Capital Required	No
Maximum Authorized Capital Investment	Unlimited
Capital Considerations	Any Currency or in Kind
Subject to Currency Controls & Restrictions	No
Application Fees	No
Annual Government Fees	**Wyoming** **Nevada**
	$100 First Year $450 First Year
	$50 Thereafter $350 Thereafter
Keeping of Accounts Required	Yes
Filing of Accounts and Returns Required	Yes
Annual Government Return Filing Fees	No
Auditing of Accounts Required	No
Re-Domicile from a Foreign State	Yes
Re-Domicile to a Foreign State	Yes
Shelf Companies Available	No
Incorporation Time	**Wyoming** **Nevada**
	3-5 Business Days 24 Hours *($125 Fee)*

Limited Liability Company (LLC)

Limited Liability Companies were created in Wyoming in 1977 and fully adopted by all states in the early 1990's. A Limited Liability Company is a "person" and has a separate legal personality. A 'single-member' LLC *(an LLC with one owner)* does not file a separate tax return, it is a disregarded entity for tax purposes and the single-owner is responsible for filing information on their personal 1040 tax return in the form of a K-1. A 'multi-member' LLC *(an LLC with more than one owner)* has the tax flexibility of filing either a 1065 'partnership' flow-through tax return or an 1120 'corporate' stand-alone tax return. The great states of Nevada and Wyoming are one of only a few states in the union wherein their state statutes specifically apply the charging protection to single-member Limited Liability Companies as the exclusive remedy to judgement creditors, and Nevada 'Series' Limited Liability Companies are arguably the best in the nation.

Types of Limited Liability Companies

'Single-Member'

Whereas a Corporation has shareholders, a Limited Liability Company has 'members' and a 'single-member' LLC has one owner. The IRS disregards a single-member LLC as a separate entity and looks to the single-member as the responsible (tax-paying) party just as most courts look to the single-member as the (liable) party.

'Multi-Member'

A 'multi-member' LLC has two or more owners and can be considered a stand alone entity by the IRS. A properly formed multi-member LLC may choose between the tax election of a 1065 'partnership' flow-through tax return or an 1120 'corporate' stand-alone tax return. In most states multi-member LLC's are considered a separate entity by the courts and afforded varying degrees of the charging order protection.

'Professional'

A Professional Limited Liability Company (PLLC) is organized for the purpose of allowing professionals such as an accountant, architect, doctor, engineer, chiropractor or lawyer to provide public services through an entity. In addition to an accredited license, some states require the formation of a PLLC to operate a professional service and generally insist that two or more professionals in the same field of expertise participate in the company. For example, two chiropractors may form and operate a Professional LLC together but a doctor practicing general medicine and a civil engineer designing roads and bridges would be prohibited from forming a Professional LLC together.

'Series'

A 'Series' Limited Liability Company is a currently available in a little over a dozen states (including Nevada, but not Wyoming). Series LLC's provide liability protection through a 'series' of subsidiary LLC's each of which segregates the assets and liabilities of one subsidiary from the other. However, *"Is a 'Series' Limited Liability Company akin to putting all your eggs in one basket or can a Series LLC truly provide asset protection through the segregation of subsidiary assets and liabilities?"*

Originally designed to assist investment companies in the mutual fund industry avoid a multitude of SEC filings, Delaware introduced special interest legislation in 1996 to enable one company to act as an 'umbrella' for the activities of all their individual client funds.

Such a strategy has been successfully implemented internationally with 'Segregated Portfolio Companies' (in the British Virgin Islands and Belize) and Protected Cell Companies (in the Republic of Seychelles) for insurance companies and other industries servicing large quantities of related clientele.

The method of shielding large institutions from mass claims arising from catastrophic events was then brought to average individuals engaged in common business activities with varying degrees of risk such as real estate investing, construction and fund raising. However, many questions have since arisen on 'how to use' a Series LLC with regards to banking, documentation and taxation.

A Series LLC consists of a 'master' company and a "series" of 'subsidiary' companies, which may conduct unrelated business activities with differing ownership interests. Of the thirteen states which have legislation enacted for a Series LLC, only Illinois requires the subsidiaries (or series) to be registered with the Secretary of State. All other jurisdictions leave the responsibility of maintaining proper books and records up to the company ownership.

Nevada added the Series LLC in 2005 and, along with a growing number of states, allows a Series LLC to enter into contracts, hold title to assets, grant security interests and to sue or be sued just like other types of entities. Although no legal cases have reached any State Supreme Court to establish a precedence for the efficacy of a Series LLC, there is over ten years of use to their credit (in Nevada).

While many states do not recognize a Series LLC, as they have not yet enacted any such Series LLC legislation in their state laws, it is possible to avoid 'foreign filing' (registering a company in another state) by combining a Series LLC with other structures like land trusts, on-the-ground 'processing centers' and third-party management companies contracted to perform certain state-specific activities.

The tax treatment of a Series LLC is also becoming clearer as their use continues to spread. A Series LLC can be formed with a single-member (not recommended) or with multiple members and, if not acting as a disregarded entity for tax purposes, may choose to file either a 1065 (partnership), an 1120 (corporate), or even an 1120-S (sub-chapter 'S') tax election.

In 2008, the IRS issued Private Letter Ruling 200803004 which ruled that the Federal tax classification for a Series LLC (whether a disregarded entity, partnership or taxable association) shall be determined for each subsidiary independently. And proposed Treasury Regulation §301.7701-1(a)(1) states subsidiaries shall likely be treated (for tax purposes) as a separate entity *regardless* of whether the subsidiary is considered an entity under local law.

**Two Primary Benefits of a Series LLC and
One Responsibility which Remains Unchanged**

The first of two benefits is the ability to form and renew only one company, as opposed to multiple entities. For example, business owners (such as real estate investors) can save thousands of dollars in annual filing fees by requiring the formation of only one company instead of 5, 10, or even 20 or more separate entities.

The second benefit is that a Series LLC only requires one tax return to be filed by the master LLC and can encompass a multitude of subsidiary LLC's with it. So long as the ownership of the Series LLC is the same throughout the master and all the subsidiaries, a Series LLC requires only one tax return (generally a 1065 or an 1120) to be filed on the master LLC.

Many small to medium-sized business owners form a 'Series' LLC as a 'multi-member' entity filing a 1065 tax election. The husband and wife, or their Revocable Living Trust, are the member(s) while their Nevada "C" Corporation (filing an 1120) acts as the managing member.

The "responsibility which remains unchanged" is that a Series LLC, which consists of a master LLC with a 'series' of subsidiary LLC's, requires that each subsidiary maintain separate books and records, operating agreements, meetings, resolutions, EIN's, bank accounts and receipts for any financial responsibilities and/or debt obligations. It is important to recall that 'substance over form' is applicable in this on-going responsibility. If it looks like a duck, walks like a duck, quacks like a duck, it's not a goat. Each subsidiary, if its separate legal personality is to be respected, must behave as a separate company.

Take these action steps into consideration when investigating the use of a Series LLC:

- Each subsidiary is a separate and distinct company from the master and keeps their own respective books and records.

- Separate EIN (Employer Identification Numbers) are obtained and maintained to segregate bank accounts of each subsidiary.

- All agreements, contracts, deeds and notes, etc are signed in the name of the respective subsidiary LLC.

- Each subsidiary name should include the name of the master in its title, thus providing notice or disclosure to the subsidiary's existence. i.e. "Subsidiary Name, a Series of (Name of Master) LLC"

- Each subsidiary is to receive proper financial capitalization with no one subsidiary co-mingling funds or ownership interest in another.

Although there are substantial savings in the number of entities which need to be formed and the amount of tax returns which need to be filed, you are not precluded from maintaining the material elements for each subsidiary company. If your Series LLC is to be treated and respected as a company with its own legal personality, then each subsidiary must behave accordingly with its business formalities being in order.

Nevada 'Series' LLC Flow-Chart

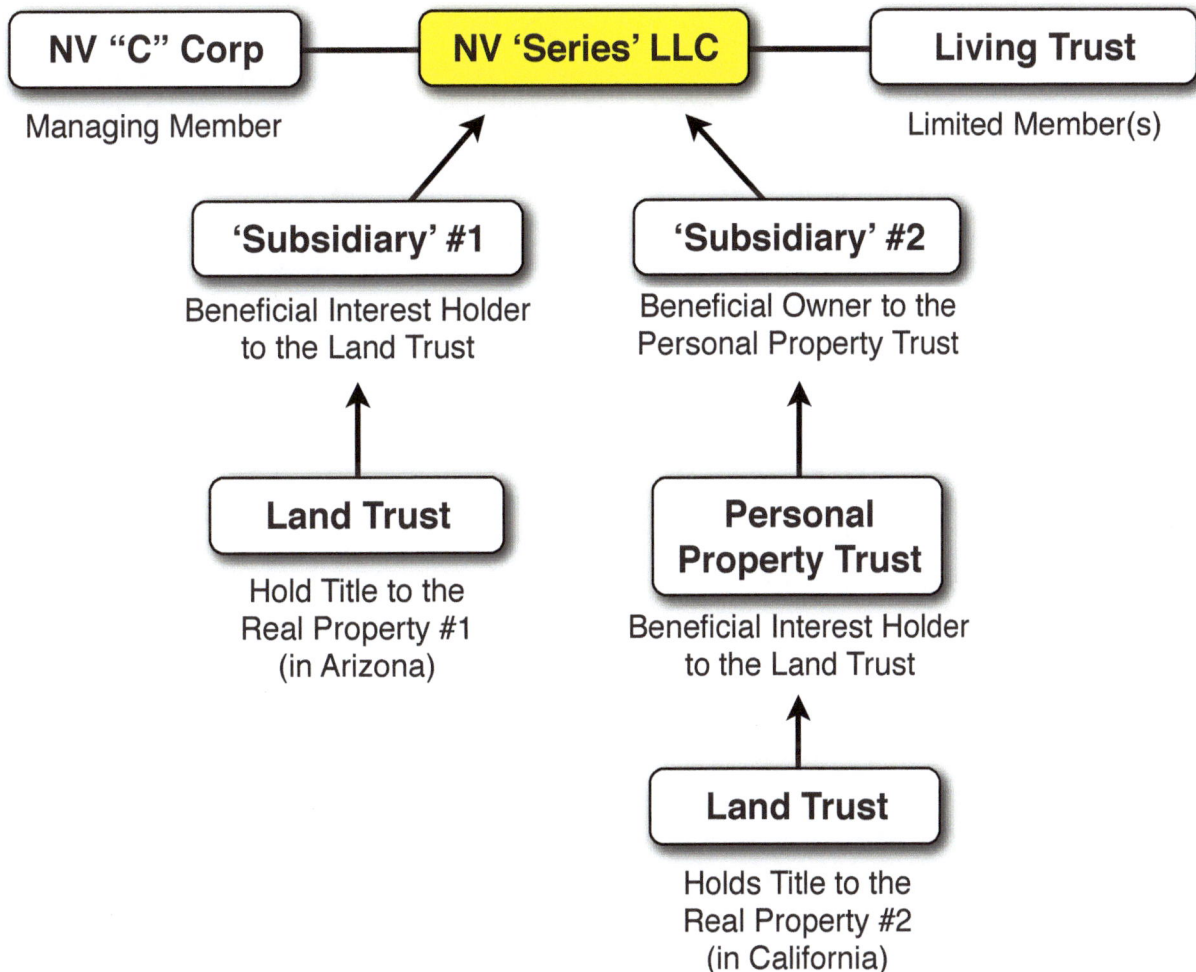

NV "C" Corp — Managing Member

NV 'Series' LLC

Living Trust — Limited Member(s)

'Subsidiary' #1 — Beneficial Interest Holder to the Land Trust

'Subsidiary' #2 — Beneficial Owner to the Personal Property Trust

Land Trust — Hold Title to the Real Property #1 (in Arizona)

Personal Property Trust — Beneficial Interest Holder to the Land Trust

Land Trust — Holds Title to the Real Property #2 (in California)

Individual Liability Protection
Nevada

Limited Liability Company
Nevada Revised Statutes (NRS)
Section 86 - Limited Liability Company
NRS 86.371 Liability of member or manager for debts or liabilities of company.
(Added to NRS by 1991, 1300; A 1995, 2112)

Unless otherwise provided in the articles of organization or an agreement signed by the member or manager to be charged, no member or manager of any limited-liability company formed under the laws of this State is individually liable for the company debts or liabilities.

Individual Liability Protection
Wyoming

Limited Liability Company
Wyoming Title 17
Chapter 29 - Wyoming Limited Liability Act
Article 3 - Relations of Members and Managers to Persons Dealing with LLC's
Section 304 - Liability of Members and Managers

(a) *The debts, obligations or other liabilities of a limited liability company, whether arising in contract, tort or otherwise:*
   (i)   *Are solely the debts, obligations or other liabilities of the company; and*
   (ii) *Do not become the debts, obligations or other liabilities of a member or manager solely by reason of the member acting as a member or manager acting as a manager.*
(b) *The failure of a limited liability company to observe any particular formalities relating to the exercise of its powers or management of its activities is not a ground for imposing liability on the members or managers for company debts, obligations or other liabilities.*

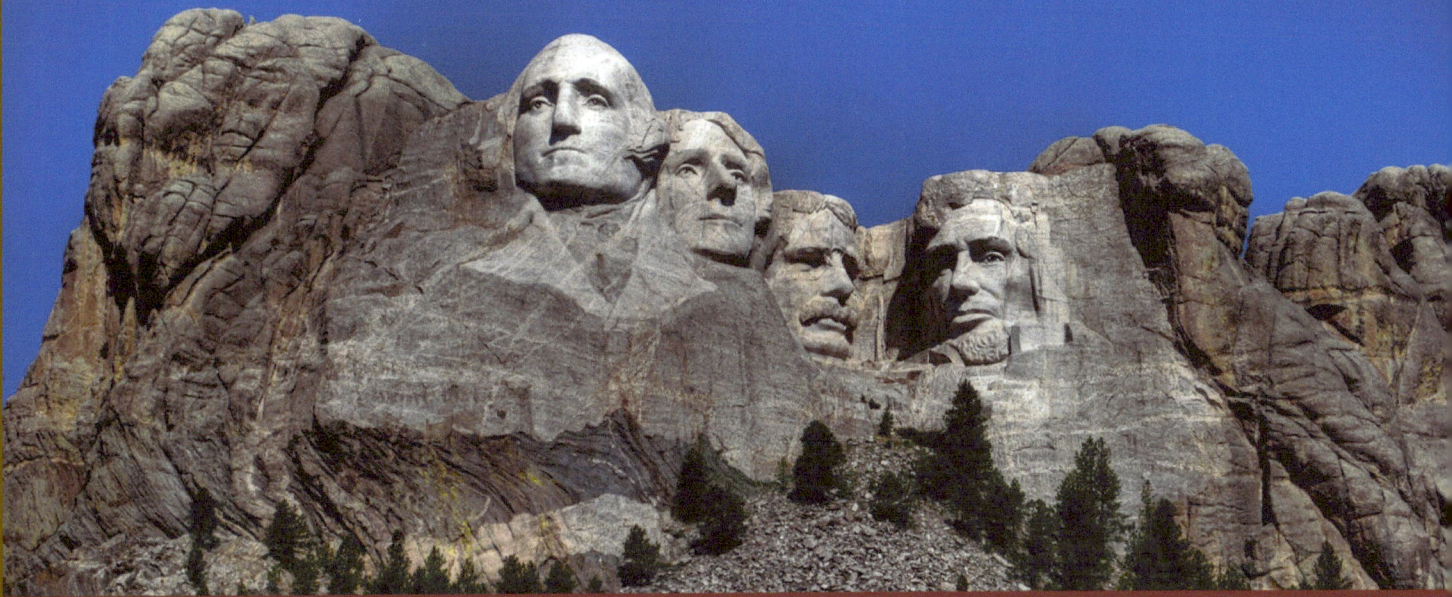

Limited Partnerships

AssetProtectionServices.com

Nevada and Wyoming Limited Partnerships

Nevada Partnership Law	Nevada Revised Statute - Chapter 87-A / 88
Wyoming Partnership Law	Wyoming Title 17 - Chapter 14
Official Document Language	English
Conduct Business Internationally	Yes
Conduct Business in United States	Yes
Conduct Business in State	Yes
Resident Agent Required	Yes
Registered Office Required	Yes
Resident Secretary Required	No
Partnership Taxation	0 % State Income Tax *(Liable Federal Tax)*
Double Taxation Avoidance Agreements	No
Tax Resident Qualification	No
Income Tax	No State Income Tax *(Corp or Individual)*
Business Tax	No
Detailed Client Application Required	No
Minimum Partners	2 *(1 General Partner and 1 Limited Partner)*
Entity Partners Allowed	Yes
Residency of Partners Allowed	Any Nationality
Register of Partners	Yes *(Secretary of State)*
Register of Partners Public Record	Yes *(But Only the General Partner)*
Disclosure of Partners to Registered Agent	Yes
Disclosure of Partners with SOS	Yes *(Nevada)*
Annual General Meeting Required	No
Partners Meeting Required	Yes *(Anywhere in the World or by Proxy)*
Partnership Resolutions	In Private Possession of Partner(s)
Partnership Seal Required	No *(But Highly Recommended)*
Minimum Paid Up Capital Required	No
Maximum Authorized Capital Investment	Unlimited
Capital Considerations	Any Currency or in Kind
Subject to Currency Controls & Restrictions	No
Application Fees	No

	Wyoming	Nevada
Annual Government Fees	$100 First Year	$450 First Year
	$50 Thereafter	$350 Thereafter

Keeping of Accounts Required	Yes
Filing of Accounts and Returns Required	Yes
Annual Government Return Filing Fees	No
Auditing of Accounts Required	No
Re-Domicile from a Foreign State	Yes
Re-Domicile to a Foreign State	Yes
Shelf Partnership Available	No

	Wyoming	Nevada
Incorporation Time	3-5 Business Days	24 Hours *($125 Fee)*

Limited Partnership (LP)

A (Family) Limited Partnership provides remarkable advantages and planning opportunities. By itself, or in combination with other techniques, the FLP can be used to create a powerful strategy for asset protection and realizing estate tax and income tax benefits. A Limited Partnership is an entity which has been recognized under law since 1916 with the creation of the Uniform Limited Partnership Act (ULPA). Enjoying almost 100 years of court precedence with all courts of the land including numerous United States Supreme Court rulings to support its foundational validity, Limited Partnerships remain one of the best ways to protect your financial interests. Comprised of two or more persons carrying on an enterprise for profit, (Family) Limited Partnerships have a 'general' partner and a 'limited' partner with varying degrees of responsibility and liability. Individuals desiring to protect assets from frivolous law suits, unwarranted creditors, thieves and liens can take advantage of the asset protection benefits afforded by Limited Partnerships.

Limited partnerships are often used as investment vehicles for large projects requiring considerable amounts of capital. Individual limited partners contributing to a venture, but not having management powers, will not have any personal liability for the debts of the business. In exchange for this protection against personal liability, a limited partner may not actively participate in management. However it is permissible for limited partners to vote on certain matters, just as shareholders have a right to vote on specific corporate matters. The partnership agreement determines whether the limited partners can vote on issues like requiring a majority vote for the sale of assets or to remove a general partner.

'General Partner'

The 'general' partner in a Limited Partnership could be likened to the general in army who, not only makes all the decisions for the army (or 'limited' partners), maintains an unlimited amount of personal liability for the debts and obligations of the limited partnership. The general partner(s) in a limited partnership are *not* afforded any charging order protection or personal liability protection in an inside lawsuit! It is essentially financial suicide for any individual to act as the general partner in an LP if the assets or activities of the limited partnership are in any way high-risk. It is advisable to instead utilize an entity (such as a Corp or an LLC) to act as the general partner in a limited partnership to assume such unlimited liability.

'Limited Partner'

'Limited' partners in a Limited Partnership are just that, they are 'limited'. A limited partner may receive profits from the partnership in consideration of their capital contribution to the partnership. Limited partners have no personal liability so long as they refrain from entering into any management or decision making processes of the LP, which would make them a *de facto* general partner. A limited partner in an LP *is* afforded charging order protection and it is therefore permissible for a limited partner to be an individual or a revocable living trust.

Types of Limited Partnerships

'Family' Limited Partnership (FLP)

Technically there is no such thing as a 'Family' Limited Partnership for, in fact, it is just a Limited Partnership where 75% or more of the partners are related by blood or marriage. The usage of the word 'Family' is more of a marketing tool than anything else and relates to the ownership of the partnership and not an entity which somehow differs from the legislation used to form a (traditional) Limited Partnership under state law. In short, the terms 'Limited Partnership' and 'Family Limited Partnership' are interchangeable and, save the ownership of the partnership, the underlying legislation upon which the entities are formed is the same as found in the Nevada Revised Statutes under Chapter 87-A and 88.

Generally, family limited partnerships hold 'safe' assets permitting parents or even grand-parents an opportunity to act as the general partner and maintain control of the family's assets without incurring any liability. If the FLP is holding onto a family business, then the husband and wife often form an LLC to act as the general partner while the limited partners are a revocable living trust, their children (or trusts created for their children) or the couple themselves. As owners of the Corporation or Limited Liability Company, which is acting in the capacity of general partner, the husband and wife are in complete control of the partnership deciding how the partnership assets are invested and whether to retain or distribute the partnership income. The husband and wife and/or grand-parents could continue to manage the family assets or family business throughout their lifetime and, upon death, control what assets pass to designated family members.

Limited Partnerships are also used as vehicles to help protect assets in prenuptial agreements or prior to filing for divorce. For example, the operating agreement can provide great clarify with regards to the ownership of assets within the limited partnership. And whereas the gift of property from a parent to a married child is the separate property of the child, when money is given the child usually spends it or commingles it with other assets which then converts to community property. If a limited partnership interest is given instead, the partnership interest cannot be commingled and remains the child's separate property. In the use of a prenuptial (and most divorces), property separate from the husband and wife is almost always awarded exclusively to the owner.

The asset protection advantages of the family limited partnership are substantial because a creditor of a limited partner may not attach any partnership asset to satisfy an individual claim against that partner. Partnerships which contain 'safe' assets and are not in debt may not be compelled to be used to satisfy the debt of any one partner. Typically, assets that have substantial value or asset which may create exposure to lawsuits are placed into one or more family limited partnerships.

'Pension' Limited Partnership (PLP)

A Pension Limited Partnership is used to hold and own your retirement funds providing protection from creditors. The Pension Limited Partnership is appropriate for cash, in-kind investments and virtually any retirement investment asset. Retirement asset funds are now exposed to creditors if you exercise any control over them or borrow from them. The Pension Limited Partnership is used to protect those assets you have set aside for your retirement in qualified deferred compensation plans such as IRA's, Keogh Plans, 401(k)'s and SEP's, etc.

A pension limited partnership is a limited partnership designed with tax deferral qualifications to continue to defer tax on those assets you have in it. The current rules may allow your creditors to take control of most types of retirement accounts. Generally, self-directed plans are more vulnerable to attacks by creditors. Since your plan assets must be reported yearly to the Department of Labor on Form 5500, the location, amount, and type of your retirement funds can easily be discovered by creditors through the discovery process and your examination under oath in a judgment debtor exam. Armed with this information, creditors may then execute on your funds, possibly leaving your planned retirement in shambles.

Because of the regulations governing related transactions with qualified retirement plans, a pension limited partnership should consider use of an independent third party to act as the general partner. The limited partner will be your pension plan, if you have multiple accounts each such account may be a limited partner. Once retirement account assets are invested in the partnership, they are protected in the same manner as described in a 'Family' Limited Partnership. Creditors are limited to obtaining Charging Orders and generally cannot compel distributions by the general partner as the pension limited partnership is housing only 'safe' assets. Once a PLP has been established, you can invest in any of the areas in which your qualified plan was previously invested domestically or internationally.

The use of the Pension Limited Partnership is extremely important because your assets are easily discoverable and generally very liquid. The Pension Limited Partnership is a major asset protection device as it is much more difficult to start over and replace pension or profit-sharing funds than other types of assets.

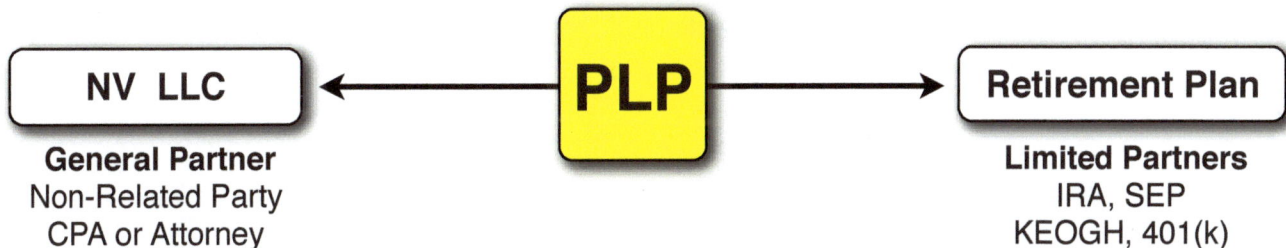

NV LLC	←	**PLP**	→	Retirement Plan
General Partner Non-Related Party CPA or Attorney				**Limited Partners** IRA, SEP KEOGH, 401(k)

PLP Illustration

If you have an IRA account or a Keogh plan, both can be controlled by yourself for investment or directed by a custodian to invest in allowable programs whether stock, bonds or otherwise. Should you be involved in a business or profession which could create exposure to potential liability and/or litigation, your investments could easily be threatened with a lawsuit and have a judgment placed against it. Thus, without taking proactive measures to properly insulate the investments, you may stand to lose all your retirement benefits to a potential future judgment creditor.

You may wish to form a Pension Limited Partnership before such a threat occurs because to transfer the funds afterwards might expose the assets to fraudulent conveyance claims in an attempt to avoid a judgement creditor. In such an event, a Court might set aside the transferred assets to the Pension Limited Partnership and give them to the creditors.

PLP Formation

A Pension Limited Partnership is formed in Nevada, a state with strong asset protection laws for limited partnerships. Select a trustworthy individual (who is independent by blood or marriage) or a company (such as a licensed or regulated professional) to act as the general partner of the PLP. Have a custodian (if not you) transfer the pension funds to the PLP as investments in the pension limited partnership. These funds (cash accounts, stocks accounts or other investments) become limited partners of the PLP in a percentage equal to their value compared with the entire value of all limited partners funds.

A separate capital account shall be maintained by the Partnership for each such limited partner. The capital account will be maintained in accordance with the capital accounting rules of Treasury Regulations Section 1.704-1(b)(2)(iv). The capital contribution of the limited partners will be in the form of cash or other assets suitable for investment in an exempt employee benefit plan, subject only to any legal prohibitions with respect to such form of capital contribution pursuant to the laws of the State used and under ERISA rules.

The terms of the Pension Limited Partnership relating to the maintenance of capital accounts are to comply with Treasury Regulations Section 1.704-1(b)(2)(iv) and shall be interpreted and applied in a manner consistent with the Regulations throughout the existence of the Pension Limited Partnership.

The General Partner should be given not less than 1% of all items of partnership income, gain, loss, deduction and credit. Such interest shall be made in accordance with Treasury Regulation Section 1.704.1. In the event there is more than one General Partner, the General Partner's share shall be divided among them. Care is to be maintained to see if the assets of the Partnership would constitute 'plan assets' under U.S. Department of Labor Regulations

2510.3-101. Then the Partnership would not be able to engage in any transaction, directly or indirectly, with a 'party-in-interest' as defined under Section 3(14)(A) of the Employee Retirement Income Security Act of 1974 or with any 'disqualified person' as that term is defined under Section 4975(e) of the U.S. Internal Revenue Code.

Only trustees or managers of qualified pension and profit sharing plans and custodians of IRA and Keogh plans may be limited partners. The limited partners, as such, shall have no powers or rights to manage the partnership. The custodian and managers of the 'limited partner' fund/investment accounts can change the investments from time to time at your request to earn, hopefully, greater returns. The profits made each year by the Pension Limited Partnership are also tax deferred.

PLP Domestic Asset Protection

If a creditor attempts to invade the Pension Limited Partnership assets, he cannot do so. He cannot execute on, attach, lien nor encumber the assets, by state law (except in Louisiana). The creditor's only remedy is to use a Charging Order which, under a IRS revenue ruling 77-137, makes him wait for a distribution of funds (if distributed). The creditor cannot interfere with the investments or the paying of the Pension Limited Partnership's bills.

PLP International Asset Protection

An even more effective protection from creditor claims and lawsuits can be achieved internationally. If your pension limited partnership uses its cash or other retirement assets in the pension limited partnership to legally buy an allowable interest in an international Limited Liability Company in, for example, St Kitts & Nevis then the pension limited partnership would own a membership interest (or 'share') of that international LLC while all of the cash and assets would now be the property of the Nevis Limited Liability Company. The only asset of the PLP would be that membership interest.

If a creditor claimed a fraudulent conveyance had occurred, and convinced a U.S. court of that, the creditor then could get into the Pension Limited Partnership. However, the only asset the creditor could get would be the membership interest of the international Limited Liability Company in Nevis. There would be no court jurisdiction over the Nevis LLC and its assets. The creditor would have to wait for a distribution from the international Limited Liability Company to satisfy his judgment. However, the Nevis LLC could invest "it's assets" for the benefit of its beneficiary, which could be a another properly structured international entity to hold, invest or re-invest the assets for your benefit.

'Tiered' Limited Partnership (TLP)

A 'Tiered' Limited Partnership is akin to a 'Family' Limited Partnership in-so-far as it makes use of its name to infer its primary purpose. A Tiered Limited Partnership utilizes more than one LP to create a multi-entity structure for a common goal but remains, at its core, an LP.

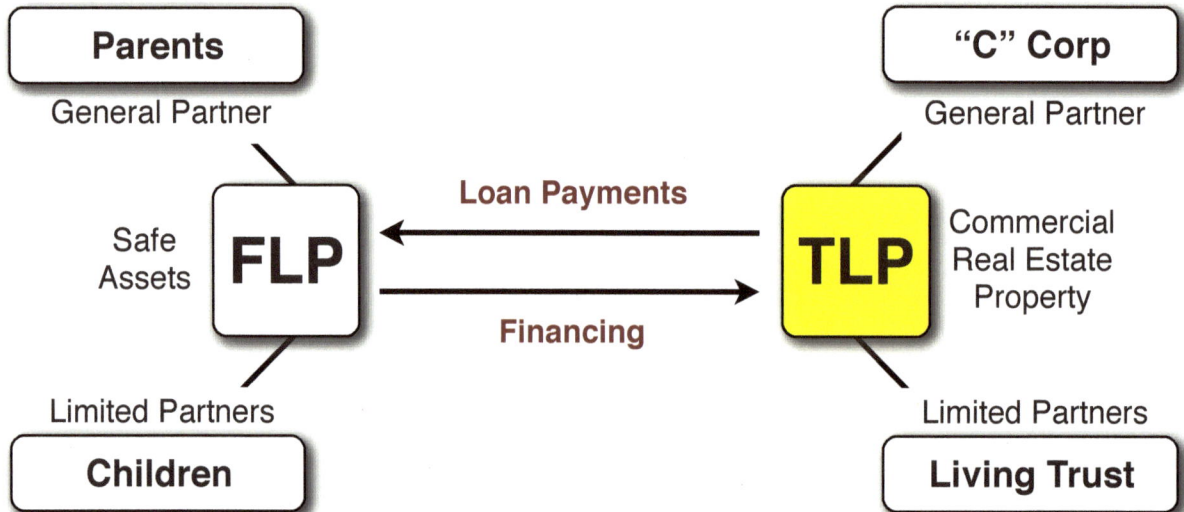

Parents		"C" Corp
General Partner		General Partner
Safe Assets **FLP**	← Loan Payments / Financing →	**TLP** Commercial Real Estate Property
Limited Partners		Limited Partners
Children		Living Trust

'Limited Liability' Partnership (LLP)

A Limited Liability Partnership is an specific entity as found in the Nevada Revised States (NRS) under 87.440 which is reserved for specific professional business endeavors such as architects, engineers, attorneys, accountants, physicians, dentists or psychiatrists, etc. If you are not a certified, licensed professional in one of these areas of practice your LLP application will be rejected by the Secretary of State.

'Limited Liability Limited' Partnership (LLLP)

A Limited Liability Limited Partnership is also a distinct type of limited partnership where the general partner has the same level of protection a limited partner receives. If an inside lawsuit were to arise, the general partner in a limited liability limited partnership would have no more liability than any limited partner in an LP or member in an LLC. The underlying legal foundation for an LLLP is found in the Nevada Revised Statutes (NRS) under 88.606 as established in 2003. Although no law suits against an LLLP have reached the higher courts (where case law or precedents are created) to solidify the validity of this type of limited partnership, after over a decade of use there are also no landmark decisions demonstrating an LLLP is anything other than a reliable asset protection entity.

Comparing Business Structures

Advantages of a Limited Liability Company or Limited Partnership over an 'S' Corporation

No Citizenship Requirements

‣ Only eligible individuals can be shareholders of an "S" corporation. Most corporations and irrevocable trusts do not qualify (with few exceptions).

‣ Any type of entity or person can be a member of an LLC or LP including a corporation, nonresident alien, ESOP, charity or another limited liability company or limited partnership.

No Membership or Partnership Limitations

‣ "S" corporations may only have up to 100 shareholders.

‣ An LLC or LP may have an unlimited number of members or partners.

No Limitations of One Class of Shares of Stock

‣ An "S" corporation can issue only one class of stock. Because of the requirement that an "S" corporation has a single class of special stock (disproportionate), distributions of cash flow or allocations of taxable income or loss are not possible.

‣ Limited liability companies may have two classes of members, such as equity and non equity interest, which may be used to distribute a capital interest to some members and an income interest to others. A limited liability company can, and has, gone public. Disproportionate distributions and allocations may be made among members of an LLC or limited partners of a limited partnership.

No Limitations on Ownership of Other Corporations

‣ "S" corporations cannot hold more than 80 percent of stock in another corporation.

‣ An LLC and LP do not have any limitation on ownership of other corporations.

No Rules on the Distribution of Property

‣ "S" corporations recognize gain upon the distribution of appreciated property. Upon the formation of an "S" corporation, the shareholders must run the Internal Revenue Code Section 251 gauntlet. In addition, gain will be recognized if the sum of the amount of liabilities assumed by the "S" corporation and liabilities to which property is subject, exceeds the shareholders' basis in the property contributed.

‣ There is no similar rule on the gain upon distribution of appreciated property for an limited liability company or a limited partnership.

No Risk of Election Termination by the Internal Revenue Service

‣ "S" corporation owners are continually at risk that the IRS will terminate their election if they fail to meet certain requirements.

‣ Limited liability companies and limited partnerships not subject to the same restriction.

Comparing Business Structures
Liability for Debts

1

	Liability for Debts	Management Participation	Transferability of Interests	Term of Existence
C Corp	All Shareholders Protected	No Restrictions	Restrictions are imposed by securities laws and by a shareholder's agreement, if any. Shareholders usually agree not to make transfers that would terminate "S" election.	Perpetual
S Corp	All Shareholders Protected	No Restrictions	Restrictions are imposed by securities laws and by a shareholder's agreement, if any.	Perpetual
LLC	All Members Protected	No Restrictions	Restrictions imposed by state laws, securities laws, and LLC Regulations, if any; generally, member may assign right to receive distributions / allocations, but assignee becomes member only if all members consent.	Varies; generally does not exceed 30 years, but can reconstitute.
LP	General partners have 100% unlimited personal liability for the debts and obligations of the LP. Limited partners are protected unless they participate in management.	Limited parters may not participate in management if they are to preserve their limited liability protection.	Restrictions imposed by state laws, securities laws, and partnership agreement; partner may assign right to receive distributions / allocations, but assignee becomes a partner only if all parters consent; partnership agreement may include restrictions on transfers to prevent or dissuade partners from readily relinquishing their partnership interests.	Unless the LP agreement stipulates otherwise, the LP shall end upon the retirement, death or insanity of the general partner.

Comparing Business Structures
Liability

2

	Liability	Interest Transferability	Asset Protection Rights Of Creditors	Ownership Rights Of Assignees
C Corp	Shareholders, directors and officers are not personally liable for the debts of the corporation unless there is fraud or severe mismanagement.	Shares are easily transferred.	Generally a judgment creditor of a shareholder can seize stock. Creditor's rights will depend on what rights and restrictions the stock carries.	May be restricted by the articles of incorporation, bylaws, or shareholder's agreement.
S Corp	Shareholders, director and officers are not generally personally liable for the debts of the corporation unless there is fraud or severe mismanagement.	Yes; But there are some IRS regulations relating to stock ownership.	Generally creditors of a shareholder can seize stock. Creditor's rights depend on rights and restrictions of the stock. However, a judgment creditor may have additional leverage if he can terminate the "S" election.	May be restricted by the articles of incorporation, bylaws, or shareholder's agreement.
LLC	Members are not liable for debts accrued by the company unless a member secured the debt personally.	Depends on the operating agreement.	Judgment creditor of a limited member may only obtain a charging order for the unsatisfied amount. To the extent so charged, the creditor has only the rights of an assignee.	Unless otherwise provided in the articles of organization or operating agreement, an assignee can become a member only if all the other members agree.
LP	General partners have 100% unlimited personal liability for the debts and obligations of the LP. Limited partners are protected unless they participate in management.	Depends on the partnership agreement.	Judgment creditor of a limited partner may only obtain a charging order for the unsatisfied amount. To the extent so charged, the creditor has only the rights of an assignee.	Unless otherwise provided in the partnership agreement, an assignee can become a partner only if all the other partners agree.

Comparing Business Structures
Qualifications

3

	Qualifications	Number of Owners	Form of Permissible Interest	Will Contribution of Appreciated Property be Taxable?
C Corp	No Restrictions	No Upper or Lower Limits	Any tangible or intangible benefit to the corporation including cash, promissory notes, services rendered, contracts for future services and other securities of the corporation.	Yes; Except if (under 351 rules) controlling 80% or more of the corporation voting power immediately after transfer.
S Corp	Various eligibility requirements, including restrictions on the number of shareholders and ownership of the subsidiaries.	No Lower Limits Upper Limit is 100	Any tangible or intangible benefit to the corporation including cash, promissory notes, services rendered, contracts for future services and other securities of the corporation.	No; Regardless of control by shareholder.
LLC	No Restrictions	Must have at least two owners to be considered a partnership for tax purposes; no upper limits. Single member LLCs (and Husband and wife ownership) are disregarded as an LLC for tax purposes.	In most states permit cash, property, services rendered, promissory notes or obligation to transfer property.	No; Regardless of control by member.
LP	Generally needs an individual general partner partner or a corporate general partner with substantial assets.	Must have at least two partners; No Upper Limits.	In most states permit cash, property, services rendered, promissory notes or obligation to transfer property.	No; Regardless of control by partner, unless recharacterized as sale or partner has net reduction in liabilities in excess of tax basis in contributed property.

Comparing Business Structures
Types of Owners

4

	Types of Owners	Filings	Name Endings	Organization Costs
C Corp	No Restrictions	Articles of Incorporation	In most states, must contain Corporation or Corp. Incorporated or Inc.	Varies by State
S Corp	Ownership is limited to U.S. citizens, residents (and green card holders) and to certain U.S. trusts. Shareholders can *not* be corporations, nonresident aliens, partnerships, limited liability companies, certain trusts or pension plans.	Articles of Incorporation	In most states, must contain Corporation or Corp. Incorporated or Inc.	Varies by State
LLC	No Restrictions	Articles of Organization	Must contain Limited Liability Company or LLC.	Varies by State
LP	No Restrictions	Certificate of Limited Partnership	Must contain Limited Partnership or LP.	Varies by State

Comparing Business Structures
Flexibility to Structure Entity

5

	Flexibility To Structure Entity	Use Of Nominee Officers/Directors	Bearer Shares Allowed	Federal Governing Act
C Corp	Unlimited	Yes	No	Model Business Corporation Act. (Note: Most states follow this act, however Nevada expanded on this act to favor businesses in operating in or from Nevada.
S Corp	Limited. Only 1 class of shares with the exception of voting or non-voting classes of shares being allowed.	Yes	No	Not applicable. "S" status is an election taken after incorporating as a "C" corporation
LLC	Unlimited	Yes	No	Uniform Limited Liability Act. Now adopted by most states. This act is also part of the US Uniform Partnership Act.
LP	Unlimited	No	No	Uniform Limited Partnership Act. Now adopted by most states. This act is also part of the US Uniform Partnership Act.

Comparing Business Structures
Managing Body

6

	Managing Body	Officers	Rules for Management of Entity	Must Formalities be Observed to Preserve Limited Liability?
C Corp	Board of Directors	Yes; Requires President and secretary.	Bylaws	Yes
S Corp	Board of Directors	Yes; Requires President and secretary.	Bylaws	Yes
LLC	Managers; unless Regulations reserve to members. All members can participate in management.	Yes; if designated by managers.	Operating Agreement	Unclear
LP	General partners; unless limited partners participate in management and relinquish their limited liability protection.	Yes; if designated by partners.	Partnership Agreement	No

Comparing Business Structures
Conduct Business in Other States

7

	Conduct Business in other States	Limited Liability of Participants Recognized in Other States	Levels of Income Tax
C Corp	Yes (By "foreign filing" in other state)	Yes	Corporate and Shareholder Level.
S Corp	Yes (By "foreign filing" in other state)	Yes	Shareholder Level Only.
LLC	Unclear in states that do not have an LLC statute.	Unclear in states that do not have an LLC statute.	Member Level Only.
LP	Yes (By "foreign filing" in other state)	Yes	Partner Level Only.

Comparing Business Structures
Pass Through of Losses and Profits

8

	Pass Through of Losses and Profits	Deductibility of Losses Attributable to Entity Debt	At-Risk Limitations
C Corp	No; preferences in distribution can be given to certain classes of stock.	Shareholders may not deduct any of the Corporation's losses as losses are taken by the Corporation prior to any dividends being paid.	Applicable if a closely-held corporation
S Corp	No; all allocations are pro-rata since only one class of stock is permitted	Shareholders may deduct the Corporation's losses only to the extent of their tax basis in their stock, which does not include any portion of the Corporations debt.	Applicable
LLC	Yes	Members may deduct LLC's losses only to the extent of their tax basis on their LLC interest, which includes their allocable share of LLC debt.	Applicable
LP	Yes	General partners only may deduct partnership losses to extent of basis, unless the limited partnership assumes the liability.	Applicable

Comparing Business Structures
Passive Activity Limitations

9

	Passive Activity Limitations	Fiscal Year	Cash Distributions	Liquidations
C Corp	Not Applicable	No Restrictions	Taxable as dividends to the extent of the Corporation's earnings and profits and then nontaxable to the extent of the shareholder's tax basis.	Taxable to both Corporation and shareholders.
S Corp	Seven Tests Apply	Generally Calendar	Generally nontaxable to the extent of the shareholders' tax basis.	Generally nontaxable at a corporate level and taxable at a shareholder level through flow-through of corporate tax items.
LLC	It is unclear whether members or managers qualify under 7 tests or only 3.	Generally Calendar	Nontaxable to the extent of a member's tax basis.	Nontaxable to the extent of the member's tax basis.
LP	Limited partner can be active under only 3 of 7 tests (i.e. Essentially the limited partner must participate in the activity for 500 hours).	Generally Calendar	Nontaxable to the extent of a partner's tax basis.	Nontaxable to the extent of the partner's tax basis.

Comparing Business Structures
Possibility of Income Allocation

10

	Possibility Of Income Allocation	Restrictions About Sources Of Income	Tax Flexibility (Profit Sharing)	Taxable on Some Fringe Benefit Plans
C Corp	No; Income is allotted only to the corporation.	No Restrictions	Yes; Not obligated to share profits through dividends.	No
S Corp	No; Income must be allotted strictly by stock ownership percentage.	Yes; Maximum of 25% of the total income may come from passive activities (dividends, rents or royalties etc.)	No; All profits (after salaries and other expenses) are shared by the shareholders during the current year.	Yes; Except employees who own 2% or less of the corporate shares.
LLC	Yes; Income can be shared among members in proportions agreed upon by the members.	No Restrictions	No; All profits (after salaries and other expenses) are shared by the members during the current year.	Yes
LP	Yes; Income can be shared among partners in proportions agreed upon by the partners.	No Restrictions	No; All profits (after salaries and other expenses) are shared by the partners during the current year.	Yes

Comparing Business Structures
Dissolution of Entity

11

	Will the Entity be Dissolved Upon Death, Retirement, Resignation, Expulsion, Bankruptcy or Dissolution of Participant?	Are Ownership Interests Securities?	Subject To Federal Income Tax at Entity Level?
C Corp	No	Shares are Securities	Yes
S Corp	No	Shares are Securities	No, however any shareholder may cause loss of tax status.
LLC	Yes; unless the Regulations provide otherwise or remaining members unanimously consent to continue the business.	Possibly not if all members have management rights.	No, if lacks transferability of interests, continuity of life or centralized management.
LP	Yes, if general partner is affected; but can be reconstituted by remaining general partner or by agreement of remaining partners.	Limited partners' interests are securities.	No; if lacks two of four corporate characteristics: 1.) limited liability 2.) free transferability of interest 3.) continuity of life 4.) centralized management

Asset Protection Services of America

Professional Strategies

Encumbering Business Assets

How do you remove the assets, equity and cash-flow from a business? Whether you are an accountant, architect, contractor, doctor, lawyer, real estate investor, stocks and bonds trader, or school teacher, you still have to contend with creating a defense against unwarranted litigation and judgement creditors while maintaining an offense for minimizing tax liabilities to build your wealth. Herein are three strategic methods for encumbering your business assets in a manner which is not overly difficult to comprehend, implement or maintain.

Protecting a Successful
High-Risk Family Restaurant

The managing members of the 'multi-member' Limited Liability Company (LLC) are the parents, and that LLC holds no real assets of which to speak (in the event of an inside lawsuit) and offers charging order protection (in the event of an outside lawsuit). The children (and/or grand-children) hold limited member interests in the LLC where they can receive passive income and have a stake in the future of the family business. The successful family restaurant business (held in the LLC) enters into a series of contracts and agreements with a Nevada Limited Partnership (with the Nevada "C" Corporation owned by the parents) to remove any value or appeal to a would-be frivolous lawsuit or judgement creditor.

Strategy 1

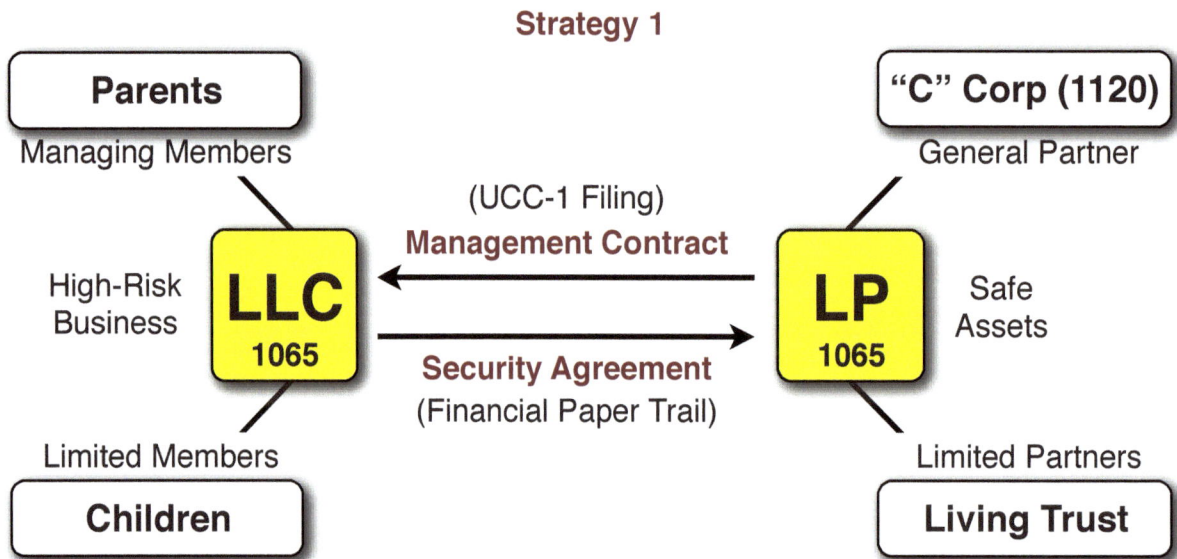

Management Contract and Security Agreement

1.) The LLC and the LP execute a management contract for the performance of managerial services which could include such things as advertising and marketing, bill-pay, bookkeeping, consulting, inventory control, payroll and tax preparation, etc. In consideration for such services the LLC would remit reasonable payments (according to fair market value) and the LP would insist the LLC execute a security agreement as collateral for the management contract in the event of a default, bankruptcy or lawsuit. The scope of the security agreement would encumber the accounts receivables, bank accounts, cash-flow and inventory of the LLC as consideration of, and to ensure timely payment for, the said services. The LP files these signed and notarized documents with a Uniform Commercial Code (UCC-1) form to create a public record of the lien.

Strategy 2

Parents		"C" Corp (1120)
Managing Members		General Partner

(UCC-1 Filing)
Financial Loan

LLC 1065 — High-Risk Business

LP 1065 — Safe Assets

Promissory Note
(Financial Paper Trail)

Limited Members		Limited Partners
Children		Living Trust

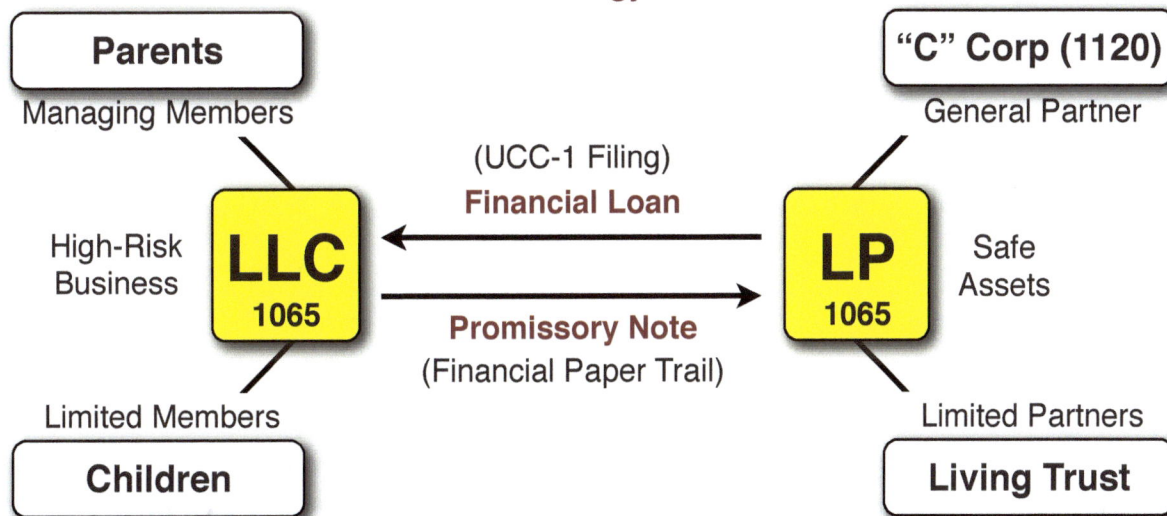

Financial Loan and Promissory Note

2.) Next, the LLC can petition the LP for a financial loan. The exact amount, nature of the loan, fixed interest rate, repayment schedule and conditions are articulated in the loan agreement. The LLC and the LP execute a promissory note for the agreed terms of repayment based on the amount of funds being lent. The LP then files these signed and notarized documents with a Uniform Commercial Code (UCC-1) form to create a public record of the lien. It is critical the LLC repay the loan according to the agreement via check or wire transfer just as it would with any other lending institution. The strength in validating the loan agreement document, as shown on the public record through the use of the UCC-1 form, is the verifiable loan payments (financial transactions) between the respective LLC and LP bank accounts.

Strategy 3

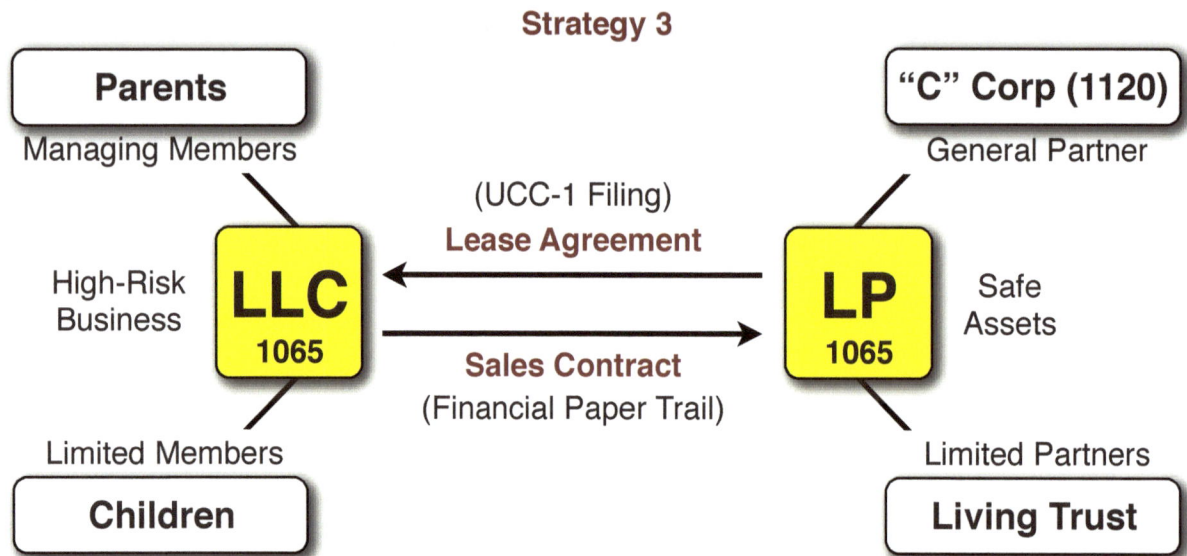

Lease Agreement and Sales Contract

3.) Lastly, the LLC can absolve itself of many of its major assets, such as large and expensive pieces of kitchen equipment like stoves, gas grills, refrigerators, freezers, walk-in coolers, pizza ovens, chicken rotisseries, salad bars, commercial dish-washers, catering equipment as well as tables, chairs and cash registers, etc (which would otherwise be subject to seizure by a judgement creditor) and sell them to LP whereby they can be rented or leased back to the LLC. The appropriate sales contract, inventory list and rental agreement would be duly executed. The LP files these signed and notarized documents with a Uniform Commercial Code (UCC-1) form to create a public record of the lien.

Conclusion

These strategies, used jointly or severely, would place the assets of the limited liability company into the limited partnership and out of the reach of judgement creditors, giving the LP debt superior 'first in line - first time' position to creditor claims. The liens would have to be satisfied in favor of the LP before judgement creditors could receive any funds.

The Limited Liability Company (LLC) and Limited Partnership (LP) are both 'flow-through' entities which file a 1065 tax return. Given the assets, equity and cash-flow of the successful high-risk family restaurant were transferred over to the limited partnership, the general parter which is a Nevada "C" Corporation would be able to business expense a vast majority of the earnings with pre-tax dollars. Any remaining profits can be retained by the "C" Corp (taxed only at the federal level) or passed onto the various family members by the LP or LLC as income in the form of a K-1 taxable at their individual income tax bracket levels.

Stock and Bond Traders

Part-time or full-time stock and bond traders have three primary options to run their business.

First   File the Form 1040 (a U.S. Individual Tax Return) which is the most expensive solution and unfortunately what most people do.

When filing a Form 1040 for your individual tax return, the ability to deduct expenses related to your investment activities is extremely limited. Certain expenses are deductible, but these itemized deductions are subject to only 2% of the adjusted gross income (AGI) limitation. Additionally, deductions for investment seminars and home offices are generally disallowed.

Another limitation affecting more and more investors is the 'Wash Sale Rule'. This rule prevents you from realizing losses on securities sales if you are in basically the same financial position in a 61-day window of time. The goal of the IRS was to prevent you from selling a position simply to record the loss, and then immediately buying back the stock at a lower basis price. Unfortunately, with active trading being more the norm, individuals often find themselves moving in and out of the same stock within the same 61-day window.

Second   File as a 'trader' and deduct your business expenses on the Schedule C of your Form 1040. This is not advisable as it does not offer you any income tax reduction strategies.

The most options are available by converting your investment activities into a trading business. Once your investing activities are recognized as a business you are able to deduct any 'ordinary and necessary' business expenses. However, in case after case, the tax courts made it crystal clear that it is nearly impossible to qualify as a trader. To qualify you would most likely have to be trading full-time, hold your positions for less than a day and trade a large amount of assets most every business day throughout the year. In essence, the court has said, *"if you're not on the floor of an exchange or holed up in a trading room, you don't qualify"* as a trader.

Some tax advisors have been very active in promoting 'trader status' filings. However, if you look at the actual text from court cases, you would likely agree that attempting to establish your trading business as an individual trader on your personal Form 1040 tax return is a risky proposition in that it could easily draw attention to an audit. The point is that while a small portion of active traders can realize substantial tax savings by filing as a 'trader', a majority of investors do not qualify and need an alternative strategy.

Third   Place your trading capital into a legal entity such a corporation, limited liability company, limited partnership or a combination thereof.

Placing your trading capital in an entity structure is a qualifying method that is automatic, trouble-free and positively overflowing with powerful tax benefits. This strategy is what business greats like Warren Buffet, Michael Dell and Michael Bloomberg, along with thousands of others, have chosen for their investment capital.

One of the most exciting things about using a "C" Corporation is the sheer amount of tax deductions and perks available to corporate owners and their employees. Congress has created tax laws and special exemptions for "C" Corporations. Even small corporate traders have found that by operating their trading business through a "C" Corporation they can legally write-off any 'ordinary and necessary' business expenses.

Such business expenses include forming your corporate entity, computers (hardware and software), home office equipment, educational expenses, costs incurred attending board meetings held in vacation areas, contributions of up to $40,000 to your own pension plan, a large percentage of meals, entertainment, travel and much more. In addition, you can grant yourself all the legal perks, benefits, tax breaks and tax deductions afforded to larger companies.

Professional Service Corporations

Professionals such as accountants, architects, dentists, lawyers and physicians struggle to find the proper balance of tax breaks, liability protection and corporate practicality. As a result, many professionals use a professional corporation (often as required by State law) to provide a degree of liability protection and tax benefits, especially with regard to pensions. But the limitation of the professional corporation is in the body of law that exists defining the relationship between the provider and recipient of a professional service. In many instances, the professional is held personally liable regardless of his or her corporate status. The solution to this problem can be found in following this innovative strategy designed specifically for professional corporations:

✓ The practicing professional forms a Professional Corporation through which the professional services are performed.

✓ A "C" Corporation or "Non-Profit" Corporation, ***not*** a 501(c)(3), is formed for the purpose of managing the practice, which will also 'own and maintain' the client base.

✓ If a "C" Corporation, the stock is issued into any combination of the following:
• Business Preservation Trust
• Revocable Living Trust
• Name of the Spouse. This is ***not*** recommended as 'divorce' is one of the most common forms of lawsuit or litigation, especially for professionals in high-stress environments, and in community property states the stock (and any other assets) issued to one spouse is owned by both parties unless specified to the contrary.

✓ Either the "C" Corporation or "Non Profit" Corporation then enters into a contractual agreement with the Professional Corporation to provide the professional services in return for a 'reasonable fee' as established according to fair market value.

✓ The clients (patients) pay the managing corporation (which is the "C" or "Non-Profit" Corporation), that handles the billing and scheduling for services rendered (by the Professional Corporation).

This simple, yet effective, structure removes the challenges inherent in defining the relationship between the provider and recipient of a professional service while providing liability protection by isolating the risk associated with the professional service from the assets of the business. If the professional is involved in a lawsuit or receives a judgment, the second corporation (the "C" Corporation or "Non-Profit" Corporation) could exercise a provision in the contract between the two companies which terminates the relationship with the Professional Corporation in the event of any such claim or suit and replaces it with another professional service provider.

Eliminating 'Provider and Recipient' Relationship Issues

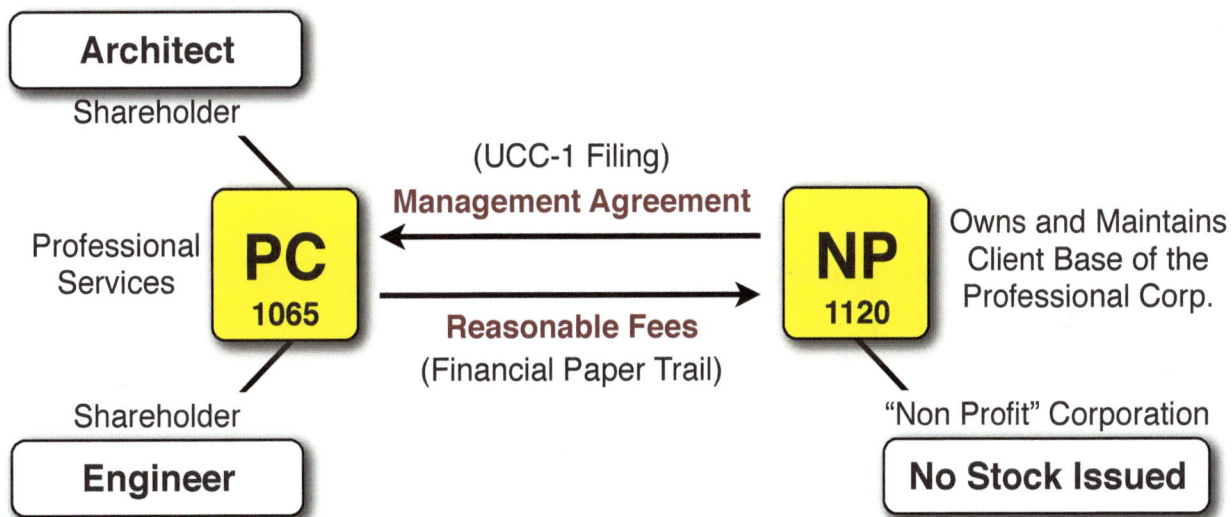

Sole Proprietorships

A Sole Proprietorship is a single person (or husband and wife) who operates a traditional brick and mortar business, internet business or home-based business (like network marketing) in an individual capacity under their personal name or under a 'dba' (Doing Business As). The Sole Proprietorship, while easy to form and operate, has a plethora of negative attributes which can be easily remedied with the formation of a "C" Corporation.

If a business has a 'brick and mortar' storefront location or employees, then forming a "C" Corporation in the state wherein the business is physically located would be appropriate. If a business has a more ethereal 'online presence' then a Nevada or Wyoming "C" Corporation may suffice, although State sales tax may be applicable for any online business transactions made with clients who reside in the respective jurisdiction. In most every state, a "C" Corporation can be formed and operated by one person just like a Sole Proprietorship, but without the drawbacks!

Audit Exposure

Sole Proprietorship   Individuals as well as Sole Proprietorships file a 1040 federal tax return and belong to the highest audited demographic by the Internal Revenue Service (IRS) and State taxing agencies.

"C" Corporation   "C" Corporations file an 1120 tax return and enjoy the lowest audited demographic by the Internal Revenue Service (IRS) and State taxing agencies. When operating a business (as a "C" Corporation), the chances of a "C" Corporation being audited is less than 1%.

Doing Business As (or 'dba') Filings

Sole Proprietorship   In order to operate a business as a Sole Proprietorship, a 'dba' (Doing Business As) notification must be filed within each county the Sole Proprietor wants to conduct business.

"C" Corporation   A "C" Corporation *only* files with the Secretary of State wherein the business was incorporated (and operated - if for some reason the "C" Corporation were conducting business in another states and needed to be 'foreign filed'). Unlike a Sole Proprietorship, a "C" Corporation can conduct business anywhere within the state under one filing with the Secretary of State and not just within one county under a 'dba'.

Lawsuits

Sole Proprietorship   If any individual or Sole Proprietorship problems result in a lawsuit, besides the time it take to litigate the suit, *all* business and personal assets are subject to seizure by a judgement creditor.

"C" Corporation   With "C" Corporations, only business assets are at risk. The personal assets of directors, employees, officers and shareholders are protected by State statute unless an individual committed fraud or (gross) negligence.

Losses

Sole Proprietorship   Individuals as well as Sole Proprietorship businesses are *only* allowed to take a tax deduction for a maximum of 25% of their losses.

"C" Corporation   "C" Corporations enjoy a tax deduction for 100% of their losses.

Pre Tax vs. After Tax

Sole Proprietorship   The taxability of the individuals and Sole Proprietorships are based on the gross (pre-tax) amount of their income. Individuals and Sole Proprietorships receive income, pay taxes and *then* make purchases (or pay bills) with any remaining 'after-tax' money.

"C" Corporation   The taxability of "C" Corporations is based on the net (after tax) amount of their income. "C" Corporations receive income, buy things (or pay bills) and *then* pay taxes on any money remaining!

Self Employment Taxes

Sole Proprietorship   The income of the Sole Proprietorship is subject to federal self employment taxes of 15.3%. In addition, *all* income of the business is considered personal income and taxed at higher rates accordingly.

"C" Corporation   "C" Corporations only pay federal unemployment taxes in accordance with FUTA (Federal Unemployment Tax Act) on the salary and bonuses it pays to directors, employees and officers. Salaries are determined by the "C" Corporation and set 'high or low'.

Tax Deductible Perks

Sole Proprietorship   The Sole Proprietorships have *very few* tax deductible perks.

"C" Corporation   "C" Corporations enjoy the widest possible range of deductible perks allowable under the Internal Revenue Code (IRC).

Tax Strategies

What is Tax Deductible?

The most frequently asked question by a new entity owners is, "What is tax deductible?" This is a challenging question to answer completely as it depends largely on you, the type of business you are in, and the manner in which you run your business. However, IRS Publication 535 helps shed some light on the subject:

IRS Publication 535

*"To be deductible, a business expense must be both 'ordinary and necessary'.
An 'ordinary expense' is one that is common and accepted in your industry.
A 'necessary expense' is one that is helpful and appropriate for your trade or business.
An expense does not have to be indispensable to be considered necessary".*

Tax Deductible Items and Medical Expense Deductions

Please see our publication entitled ***"Bookkeeping in About an Hour"*** for a complete breakdown on over a hundred verifiable tax deductible items and medical expense deductions and complete details on how to account for it all!

Bookkeeping in About an Hour

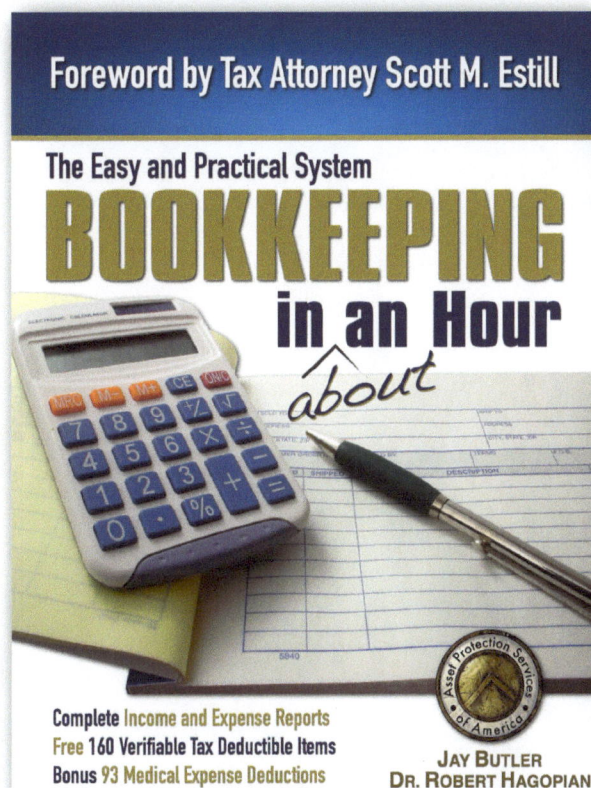

Foreword by Tax Attorney Scott M. Estill

The Easy and Practical System

BOOKKEEPING in about an Hour

Complete Income and Expense Reports
Free 160 Verifiable Tax Deductible Items
Bonus 93 Medical Expense Deductions

JAY BUTLER
DR. ROBERT HAGOPIAN

IRS Filing Guide

Individuals, Sole Proprietorships and 'Single-Member' LLC's
('Single-Member' LLC's are Disregarded Entities from a Tax Perspective)
- File a Schedule C *(trade or business activities)*
- File a Schedule E *(rental real estate activities)*
- Carry profits or losses on Form 1040.

Limited Partnerships and 'Multi-Member' LLC's Taxed as a Partnership
(Including Multi-Member 'Series' LLC's)
- File Form 1065
- Report partner and member income and expenses on Form K-1.

"C" Corporations and 'Multi-Member' LLC's Taxed as a Corporation
- File Form 1120
- File Form 1120-A only if filing Form 8832 *(treated as an association)*
- Report dividends to shareholders on Form 1099-DIV and is include on Schedule B.
- Report "PS 58" costs for insurance benefits in Box 12 of Form W-2.

"S" Corporations
- File Form 1120-S and report shareholder income and expenses on Form K-1.

IRS Resources

IRS Publication 335
- Tax Guide for Small Business

IRS Publication 463
- Travel, Entertainment, Gift, Car, Expenses

IRS Publication 535
- Business Expenses

IRS Publication 536
- Net Operating Losses

IRS Publication 541
- Partnerships

IRS Publication 542
- Corporations

IRS Publication 583
- Starting a Business and Keeping Records

IRS Publication 3402
- Limited Liability Companies

IRS 1099 Filing Requirements

*The filing requirements with the IRS generally require you to file Form 1099 on any of the following activities during the previous calendar year:

➡ any independent contractor who's worked for your business and to whom you have paid $600 or more;
➡ any partnership you've paid more than $600 for work done for your business;
➡ any corporation that you've paid $600 or more for legal or medical services;
➡ anyone you've paid more than $600 in rent - whether for space or for equipment - unless they're a corporation or real estate agent;
➡ anyone you've paid more than $600 in interest in the course of your trade or business;
➡ anyone you've paid more than $10 in royalties;
➡ any attorney you paid more than $600 in the course of your trade or business.

The filing requirements with the IRS generally require you do **not** need to file Form 1099 on any of the following activities:

➡ employees require you file a W-2 for them;
➡ corporations that have done work for you, except for legal or medical as noted above;
➡ independent contractors whom you've paid less than a total of $600 during the previous calendar year;
➡ work performed for you personally rather than for a business;
➡ any payments made to tax-exempt organizations.

Although non-profit organizations must file a Form 1099, your for-profit company does not have to file for payments made to charitable organizations or government entities.

*Remember the IRS charges a penalty for not filing a Form 1099.

IRS Filing Calendar

January 15	Due date of the fourth and final installment of the previous year's estimated tax for individuals (unless you file your previous year's tax return and pay any balance due by January 31).
January 31	Employers must furnish the previous year's W-2 statements to employees. 1099 information statements must be furnished to payees by payers.
January 31	Employers must file the previous year's federal employment (Form 941) and unemployment (Form 940) tax returns and pay any tax due.
February 28	Payers must file information returns (such as 1099s) with the IRS. (March 31 is the deadline if filing electronically).
February 28	Employers must send W-2 copies to the Social Security Administration.(March 31 is the deadline if filing electronically).
March 15	The previous calendar year corporation income tax returns are due.
March 15	Deadline to request 6 month extension of time to file corporate income tax returns. Taxes are due regardless of extension filing.
April 15	Individual income tax returns for the previous year are due.
April 15	Deadline to request a 6 month extension of time to file personal income tax returns and/or partnership and LLC income tax returns. Taxes are due regardless of extension filing.
April 15	The previous year's partnership and LLC income tax returns are due.
April 15	The previous year's annual gift tax returns are due.
April 15	Deadline for making your current year's IRA and education savings account contributions.
April 15	First installment of the current year's individual estimated tax is due.
April 30	Employers must file Form 941 for the first quarter of this year's taxes.
June 15	Second installment of this year's estimated tax is due.
July 31	Employers must file Form 941 for the second quarter of this year's taxes.
September 15	Third installment of this year's estimated tax is due.
September 15	Deadline for filing your previous year's corporation tax return if you filed an extension on the March 15 deadline.
September 15	Deadline for filing your previous year's partnership and LLC tax return if you filed for an extension on the April 15 deadline.
October 15	Deadline for filing your previous year's individual income tax return if you filed for an extension on the April 15 deadline.
October 31	Employers must file Form 941 for the third quarter this year's taxes.

1120 Tax Elections

Taxation for Entities Filing an 1120 Tax Election
Including "C" Corporations and 'Multi-Member' Limited Liability Companies

"C" Corporations, or LLC's filing an 1120, pay tax on their income at corporate rates *[IRC § 11(b)]* and are entitled to take many tax deductions not available to individuals, "S" Corporations, Limited Liability Companies (filing a 1065 partnership flow-through return) and most trusts. With an "S" Corp or an LLC (filing a 1065) all of the corporate or company income flows (or is passed) onto the 1040 tax return of the shareholders or members which can push the owners 'up' into a higher tax bracket. "C" Corporations, or LLC's filing an 1120, have a lower federal tax rate at all levels of income up to $250,000 with a structure ranging from 15% on the first $50,000 of *net* income (money left over after all expenses have been paid) to as much as 39% in the highest income tax brackets. On average, entities filing an 1120 tax election pay 22.25% on the first $100,000 of earnings and less than 31% on the first $200,000.

Accumulated Earnings Tax

An Accumulated Earnings Tax penalizes corporations for amassing cash reserves in order to avoid income taxes avoid double taxation by leaving money in the corporation. Retaining earnings may work for a while, but will eventually face a 15% Accumulated Earnings Tax.

Adjusted Net Income

✓ Adjusted Net Income (for Schedule D) includes:
  • gross income from any unrelated trade or business;
  • gross income from functionally related businesses;

- interest payments received on loans;
- amounts received or accrued as repayments of amounts taken as qualifying distributions for any tax year;
- amounts received or accrued from the sale or disposition of property to the extent acquisition of the property was treated as a qualifying distribution for any tax year;
- any amounts set aside for a specific project to the extent the full set aside was not necessary for the project;
- interest on government obligations excluded under section 103 of the Code;
- net short-term capital gains on sale or other disposition of property; and income received from an estate if the estate is considered terminated for income tax purposes because of a prolonged administration period.

Adjusted Net Income (for Schedule D) does *not* include:
- gifts, grants, and contributions received;
- long-term capital gains or losses;
- net section 1231 gains;
- capital gain dividends;
- the excess of fair market value over adjusted basis of property distributed to the U.S. or a possession or political subdivision, a state or its political subdivision, a charitable trust or corporation for public purposes, or income received from an estate during the administration period.

In computing adjusted net income, deduct the following: ordinary and necessary expenses paid or incurred for the production or collection of gross income, or for the management, conservation, or collection of gross income (includes operating expenses such as compensation of officers, employee wages and salaries, interest, rent, and taxes); straight-line depreciation and depletion (not percentage depletion); and expenses and interest paid or incurred to carry tax-exempt obligations. Do not deduct net short-term capital losses for the year in which they occur (these losses cannot be carried back or carried over to earlier or later tax years); the excess of expenses for property used for exempt purposes over the income received from the property; charitable contributions made by you; net operating losses; and special deductions for corporations.

Borrowing Money

You can borrow up to $10,000 tax-free from the corporation *[IRC §7872(c)(3)(A)]* so long as you show a business purpose other than avoiding tax *[Regs. §1.7872-5T]*. Should you borrow more than $10,000, you need to pay interest at least equal to the applicable federal rate ("AFR") or pay tax on the difference between your rate and the AFR. *[IRC § 7872(a)(1)]*

Business Losses

LLC's (filing a 1065) and "S" Corporations are allowed to deduct their business losses, subject to a 25% passive loss rule which leaves 75% of such losses to be absorbed by you! But should your company be structured as a "C" Corporation, or an LLC filing an 1120, you can deduct up to 100% of the business losses.

Dividends

A dividend is a distribution of the corporation's profits to its shareholders. Generally, an entity filing an 1120 may distribute three types of dividends:

Cash Dividend — Payment of money.
Share Dividend — Distribution of additional shares of stock in the corporation.
Property Dividend — Distribution of tangible property such as real estate, stock from other corporations or inventory also known as an "in kind" distribution.

Double Taxation

One of the potential pitfalls of using a "C" Corporation is the possibility of running into the double taxation trap. As a corporation generates income, it deducts all its 'ordinary and necessary' expenses and pays tax on the taxable portion of the proceeds at the applicable corporate tax rate. 'Double Taxation' is where after-tax earnings of a "C" Corporation, or LLC's filing an 1120, are distributed to shareholders or members as non-deductible dividends.

If, after all salaries, bonuses and expenses have been paid, the company has a profit there is going to be a taxable event. The size of the taxable event depends upon what the company intends to do with the profits. If the corporation keeps the profits as reserves to finance some new project or development, it will pay the appropriate corporate income taxes on the remaining portion only.

If the corporation wants to declare a dividend to the shareholders (often expected by the shareholders), the income will be taxed twice. First it will be taxed as corporate profits at the appropriate corporate income tax rate then it will be taxed as personal income to the shareholders, subject to their respective personal tax rates. What is worse, when a corporation declares a dividend, it is not a deductible business expense for the corporation.

Entities filing an 1120 tax election can retain after-tax profits or pay them to shareholders as dividends. Double taxation is not an issue if you 'zero out' profits with legitimate business deductions and/or pay 'reasonable compensation' such as a salary or bonus. These tax strategies avoid corporate tax as long as your salary or bonuses fall under "reasonable compensation" for the services provided *[Regs. § 1.162-7(b)]*.

Paying a dividend is optional, even if the corporation has net income remaining in the bank, entities filing an 1120 tax election must still 'declare' a dividend is to be paid. But should a dividend *not* be paid to the shareholders, the corporation can hold the funds in its corporate bank account where it is taxed as 'retained earnings'. For smaller corporations, limited liability companies (filing an 1120) and/or non-publicly traded corporations with earnings of up to $5 Million, there are so many legitimate ways to 'expense' the earnings that entities filing an 1120 tax election are generally taxed only once.

Employee Benefits

Of the many benefits a "C" Corporation or an LLC filing an 1120 enjoys, one is providing lucrative employee benefit programs which are tax-deductible to the corporation and tax-free to its employees. Childcare, education, life insurance, medical and retirement plans are just a few of the types of such benefits available only to entities filing an 1120 tax election. The tax-free status for many of these plans is much less generous for people owning more than 2% of "S" Corporation stock or an LLC membership that is the shareholder or employee of a "C" Corporation.

Employee Benefit Plans

Changes in the tax laws have created a surge in the popularity of employee benefit plans in recent years. While not providing cash directly, these plans have the indirect benefit of eliminating the need for employee/owners to pay out of pocket for the same benefits. Additionally, if the plan qualifies, the corporation can deduct the contributions or expenses as they are made, rather than later. Such employee benefit plans can include:

- Employee Stock Ownership Plans (ESOP's)
- Group life and accident insurance
- Health Insurance
- Medical and dental reimbursement plans
- Professional financial planning assistance
- Retirement plans
- Stock option plans

Tab K: Employee Benefit Plans

Fringe Benefits Comparison Chart

	Employee Benefits		Who is Considered an Employee?				
Benefit	**Description**	**Provision**	**Non-Owner Employee**	**Self-Employed Individual** [3]	**Partner** [2]	**2% S Corporation Shareholder** [1]	**C Corporation Shareholder** [1]
Accident and Health Insurance	Cost of accident and health insurance provided to employee.	Tax free to the employee, subject to certain restrictions.	✔				✔
Adoption Assistance	Expenses connected with the legal adoption of an eligible person.	Employer-paid expenses are tax free to the employee, within certain dollar limits and an AGI phase-out range.	✔			✔ 9	✔ 9
Cafeteria Plans	Two or more benefits consisting of cash and qualified benefits that the employee can select.	Tax free or tax deferred to the employee.	✔				✔
Day Care Services	Expenses for the care of a dependent while the employee is at work.	Employees can pay for day care costs with pre-tax earnings or employer contributions.	✔	✔	✔	✔	✔
Deferred Compensation	Employee agrees to work now and defer receipt of salary until a future date.	May be tax deferred or taxable to the employee depending on conditions.	✔			✔	✔
De Minimis Fringe	Minimal benefits, such as occasional personal use of office equipment by employee.	Tax free to the employee.	✔	✔	✔	✔	✔
Educational Assistance	Educational costs, such as tuition, fees, books, supplies, etc. Education does not have to be job related.	Employer assistance payments of up to $5,250 are excluded from the employee's gross income.	✔ 7, 9	✔ 9	✔ 9	✔ 9	✔ 9
Employee Achievement Awards	Tangible personal property, such as a watch, given to an employee for length of service or safety achievement.	Tax free to the employee up to a specified dollar limit.	✔ 8		✔	✔	✔
Employer-Provided Vehicle	Cost of vehicle used by the employee for business or personal purposes.	May be taxable or tax free to the employee depending on conditions.	✔		✔	✔	✔
Group Term-Life Insurance	Cost of term life insurance provided to the employee.	Up to $50,000 of coverage tax free to the employee.	✔				✔
Job Placement Assistance	Cost of providing counseling on interviewing skills, resume preparation, secretarial services, etc.	Tax free to the employee unless the benefit is conditional or received in lieu of some other taxable benefit.	✔			✔	✔
Meals and Lodging	Meals and lodging provided to the employee on the employer's business premises.	Tax free to the employee if furnished on the business premises, furnished for the employer's convenience and for lodging only—as a condition of employment.	✔				✔

No-Additional-Cost Service	Hotel accommodations, telephone services, and transportation by aircraft, train, bus, subway and cruise liner.	Value excluded from the employee's gross income if service is offered to public and employer incurs no additional cost by offering the service to the employee.	✔ 4, 6		✔ 10	✔	✔
On-Premises Athletic Facilities	Athletic facilities on the employer's business premises.	Tax free to the employee if the facility is generally only used by employees, their spouses, children, etc.	✔ 4		✔ 10	✔	✔
Qualified Employee Discounts	Goods and services the employer generally offers to the public.	The value of discounted price offered to the employee is tax free to the employee when certain conditions are met.	✔ 4		✔ 10	✔	✔
Qualified Moving Expense Reimbursement	Amount received as payment or reimbursement for expenses which would be deductible under Section 217 if paid by the individual employee.	Tax free to the employee.	✔		✔	✔	✔
Qualified Retirement Plans	Employer and/or employee contributions to an employer-sponsored retirement plan.	Tax deferred to the employee until funds are withdrawn.	✔	✔ 11	✔	✔	✔
Qualified Transportation Fringe	Employer-provided commuter vehicle transportation between the employee's residence and place of employment, transit passes and qualified parking.	Exclude up to $100 per month for transit passes and employer-provided transportation; $195 (for tax year 2004) per month for qualified parking.	✔				✔
Working Condition Fringe	Goods and services the employer generally offers to the public.	Tax free to employee if it would have been deductible as a business expense had the employee paid for the goods or services.	✔ 5	✔	✔	✔	✔
Retirement Planning Services	Retirement planning advice to the employee and/or spouse.	Tax free to the employee.	✔			✔	✔

1   Assumes S and C corporation shareholders are providing services as employees.
2   A partner who provides services for the partnership.
3   An independent contractor who performs services for another company.
4   Includes any individual currently employed by the employer, the spouse and dependent children of the employee, any individual who was formerly employed by the employer and separated due to retirement or disability, and the surviving spouse of an employee who died while employed or after separation due to retirement or disability.
5   Includes currently employed employee, and any director of the employer.
6   Special rule for parents in the case of air transportation.
7   Includes any currently employed person, retired, disabled or laid-off employee and any employee presently on leave (for example, armed forces).
8   Safety achievement awards cannot go to managerial, administrative, clerical or other professional employees.
9   Not more than 5% of amounts paid by the employer during the year may be provided to more-than-5% owners (including their spouses and children).
10 Includes the spouse and children of the partner.
11 An independent contractor can participate in his or her own plan, but cannot participate in another company's plan as an independent contractor of that company.
Note: The cost of employee fringe benefits is generally tax deductible to the employer, and tax free or tax deferred to the employee when certain requirements are met.

Employee Benefits Available
Only to Entities Filing an 1120

The cost of the following employee fringe benefits is generally tax deductible to the employer and tax-free or tax deferred to the employee when certain requirements are met.

Accident and Health Insurance

Cost of accident and health insurance provided to employee. Tax-free to the employee, subject to certain restrictions.

Cafeteria Plans

Two or more benefits consisting of cash and qualified benefits that the employee can select. Tax-free or tax deferred to the employee.

Qualified Transportation Fringe

Employer-provided commuter vehicle transportation between the employee's residence and place of employment, transit passes and qualified parking. Exclude up to $100 per month for transit passes and employer-provided transportation; $195 per month for qualified parking.

Group Term-Life Insurance

Cost of term life insurance provided to the employee. Up to $50,000 of coverage tax free to the employee.

Meals and Lodging

Meals and lodging provided to the employee on the employer's business premises. Tax free to the employee if furnished on the business premises, furnished for the employer's convenience and for lodging only—as a condition of employment.

Employee 401(k) Plans

Many corporations take advantage of 401(k) plans, which, essentially is a salary reduction mechanism that reduces immediate income tax by deferring the tax on the retirement portion.

Employee Pension Plans

Entities filing an 1120 tax election have a variety of options with regards to retirement plans and pension plans. A well-designed pension plan can serve as a tax deduction tool for the company and as a tax-deferred nest egg that can compound over time for employees. Pension plans are often promoted with the term 'tax-free' in describing the pension product but, technically, that is incorrect as the proper term is 'tax-deferred'.

"C" Corporations, or LLC's filing an 1120, take their tax deduction when pension contributions are made to the plan, while income taxes on initial contributions, and the interest and dividend earnings pensions generate, are not taxed until cash is withdrawn from the fund. Upon retirement of an employee, the amounts withdrawn are taxed at the appropriate rate. Usually, the withdrawal takes place in the period of an employee's life when they are in a lower tax bracket as compared to their previous years of active employment. So, any taxes that are eventually paid are, in actuality, generally less than would have otherwise been paid.

The benefits of compounding retirement funds without tax consequences are substantial. Fund grows faster and earn higher interest than comparable investments taxed each year. It is possible the value of tax-deferred contributions and interest could amount to 500% more than if taxes were paid immediately on the contributions and interest. One drawback to establishing some pension plans is the expense in time and money required to administer the funds. Government approval and reporting may be required, along with extensive bookkeeping and supervision. Some companies find themselves having to hire an actuary in-house to keep up with the reporting demands and remain compliant.

Simplified Employee Pension (SEP) Plans

Simplified Employee Pension (SEP) plans provide an avenue for employees to save for retirement on a tax-deferred basis without the degree of paperwork, administration fees and time other plans require. SEP plans offer a level of flexibility smaller companies need. For instance, most pension plans require the employer make specified contributions each year, but SEP plans allows for employers to skip a year if earnings are poor or delay the contribution until after their corporate tax return liabilities have been discharged with the IRS.

A SEP is somewhat like an Individual Retirement Account (IRA) because each employee makes their own decision about their particular investment vehicle, such as banks, mutual funds, bond funds or brokerage house accounts. The corporation essentially finances an IRA for each employee, but is no longer is responsible for the supervision or performance of the retirement fund. There are no complicated nondiscrimination rules with which to comply; all the corporation does is make the contribution.

A significant difference between a SEP and an IRA is that an IRA limits the annual contribution to $3,000 per year. With a SEP, the contribution is based on a percentage of the employee's compensation for that year and the percentage of contribution can be changed from year to year. The maximum contribution an employee may make to a SEP is 15% of his or her wages up to $24,000. The contributions from the corporation are tax deductible and yet are not subject to Social Security or unemployment taxes. There is a 10% penalty if the funds are withdrawn before age 59.5 years of age and you are required to begin withdrawing the funds upon 70.5 years of age. A SEP can be set up easily using the IRS model (Form 5305-SEP) which contains all of the rules for the employees and the employer. And, oddly enough, the form is not sent into the IRS, it is just kept on file.

Employee Keogh Plans

A Keogh plan is the name given in honor of New York Congressman Eugene J. Keogh for having passed legislation which created a type of retirement plan for self-employed individuals and small businesses. Keogh plans are available to anyone with self-employment income, so anyone who receives a paycheck from a corporation does not qualify. However, to the degree that freelance income is earned from the corporation for work done outside the role of an employee, exists an eligibility to participate.

To set up a Keogh, there are a wide variety of IRS approved plans available at banks, financial institutions and insurance companies. Approval for these plans, or ones developed by your own corporation, require a determination letter from the IRS. As long as the Keogh plan is set up by the end of the calendar year, you have until the tax deadline of April 15th to complete the contribution.

There are two kinds of Keogh plans being 'defined contribution' and 'defined benefit' plans. Under a defined contribution plan, if you are an employee of a sole proprietor the maximum contribution is the lesser of 25% of the self-employment income up to $30,000. If you are self-employed, the maximum contribution is the lesser of $30,000 or 20% of compensation. The minimum amount you must contribute in either case is 1% of compensation. With a defined benefit plan, you have a maximum annual benefit of $130,000 upon retiring at the Social Security age of retirement. Or, to figure out how much you need to contribute to get the "defined" benefit, take 100% of the average of your three best earning years.

Employee Stock Ownership Plans (ESOP)

Stock option bonus plans are commonly used in executive compensation packages. However the value in receiving additional stock dissipates entirely with most closely held corporations if the executive is a shareholder of the company and has 100% ownership. An ESOP is the most widely known type of stock option plan. It has evolved from a novel academic concept into a sophisticated tool of corporate finance that is well-integrated into the mainstream of the American business community. Many publicly held corporations have used ESOP's as an employee benefits tool, as a takeover defense measure, and as a means of going private. Owners of closely held companies have used ESOPs not only for ownership succession and capital formation, but as an exit strategy.

An ESOP consists of a trust designed primarily to invest in and hold stock issued by the corporation for participating employees. Generally the stock held by the trust must be traded in an established market, but that is not always possible for closely held companies. In such cases, the law provides for corporate stock (which is used instead of publicly traded stock) that has voting and dividend rights at least equal to the highest available in common stock.

A corporation contributes stock to an ESOP and takes a tax deduction for its value, up to 25% of the employee's compensation or $30,000. These limits may be increased to the lesser of $60,000 or the amount of stock contributed to the plan. The stock is held in an account for each participating employee, who is allowed to control the voting of his or her shares.

When to Use an ESOP

An Employee Stock Option Plan may be a better method of corporate finance than a sale, merger or public offering for the following reasons:

- If you sell your company to another company, you will pay immediate capital gains tax, lose control and probably not be able to retain any residual equity.

- If you sell your stock to the public, you will incur an immediate capital gains tax, become subject to the jurisdiction of the Securities and Exchange Commission (SEC) and risk possible loss of corporate control.

- If you enter into a tax-free merger the capital gains tax will be deferred, but you will lose control and still have all your eggs left in one basket of stock.

If you sell to an ESOP, you can defer the federal capital gains tax, maintain control of the company, retain residual equity and invest the proceeds in a diversified portfolio of stocks and bonds without incurring a capital gains tax - all while rewarding the loyal people who helped you build the business. The corporation (as a person) benefits from this in many ways too. In addition to the tax deductions, the ESOP is able to generate capital through tax-deductible loans. The corporation's deductible cash contributions to the ESOP are used by the ESOP to repay loans which were used to buy the diversified corporate stock.

Additional ESOP Advantages

✔ An ESOP can borrow to purchase stock contributed to the plan, even if the stock is purchased directly from the corporation. The loan can be used to purchase more stock than is needed for contributions to the plan and the balance of the proceeds can be used for annual expenses.

✔ Any lender to an ESOP is able to receive 50% of the interest tax-free.

✔ The corporation can claim a deduction for dividends paid on its stock held in an ESOP if the dividends are paid in cash directly to participants within 90 days of the end of the plan year, or the dividends are used to repay a loan used to purchase additional stock.

✔ The corporation can get a deduction for ESOP contributions of company stock without cash outlay.

✔ Employees are motivated and productive, enhancing the value for every shareholder.

These benefits are achievable as a result of Internal Revenue Code Section 1042, which provides a road map for the tax-free rollover of proceeds from the sale of stock to an ESOP. The ESOP is required to purchase 30% or more of the common equity in the corporation and that the seller has had at least a three-year holding period. The seller must reinvest the proceeds in other US domestic securities within a 12 month period.

Estimated Taxes

Entities filing an 1120 tax election *not* earning 'large amounts' of income may disregard the requirement to make quarterly payments if its estimated tax (income tax minus deductions) are reasonably small. If "C" Corporations or LLC's filing an 1120 earning 'large amounts' of income fail to make payment on such installments when due, it may be subject to an under payment penalty.

Fiscal Year-End

Individuals, "S" Corporations and LLC's filing a 1065 return report their taxable income based on the January 1 to December 31 calendar year and are allowed no real opportunity to shift income between calendar years. It is possible for an "S" corporation to make a section 444 election, which generally allows for a tax year ending on September 30, October 31, or November 30, but estimated tax payments must be made that offset any advantage a shareholder might gain by having an offsetting fiscal year. However, another useful tool in the tax-game arsenal of the "C" Corporation, or an LLC filing an 1120, is the ability to shift income between calendar years and to close their fiscal year at the end of any calendar month. The IRS default year-end is December 31st but may be amended with the submission of IRS "Form 1128". We usually recommend you pick a fiscal quarter such as March, June, or September in order to have some fluidity with the rest of the business community. Having your corporate year end on a fiscal quarter generally makes bookkeeping and accounting easier too. June enables you to have six months on either side of the calendar to move money around and consider your expense options before earnings becomes taxable income. The first tax return will almost always be less than 12 full calendar months, so don't worry about coordinating the first year's tax filing with the incorporation date.

Gross Investment Income

As defined in section 509, gross investment income means the gross amount of income from interest, dividends, payments with respect to securities loans, rents, and royalties, but not including any such income to the extent included in computing the tax imposed by IRS section 511.

Gross Receipts

Gross receipts includes monies earned from activities related to your charitable or other section 501(c)(3) activities, such as selling admissions or merchandise, performing services, or furnishing facilities.

Group Life and Accidental Insurance

Premiums on group life insurance are deductible expenses to entities filing an 1120. They are also excluded from inclusion in the employee's taxable income if the insurance coverage provided is less than $50,000 for that employee. If the employee has coverage greater than that amount, the portion of the premium for the excess will be subject to tax. For a group term life insurance plan to qualify for the employee exclusion, it must cover at least ten (10) full-time employees or, if the company has less than 10 employees, all insurable employees must be covered. The plan must also meet the nondiscrimination requirements of the Tax Code.

Health Insurance

Employer-paid health insurance premiums are excluded from an employee's gross income. However, the tax treatment of benefit claims depends upon the type of coverage for which the corporation paid. The employee is taxed on disability benefits that are based on the duration of work missed. But the employee can exclude from his gross income any reimbursements he receives for medical expenses.

Income Splitting

Legitimately hiring family members to work for a "C" Corporation or LLC filing an 1120 tax election can take deductible dollars out of the corporation or company and, as long as the family members are actually performing the work and the salary is reasonable and commensurate for the position, the compensation is deductible. This technique is called 'income splitting'. Income splitting can keep income in the family at a lower tax rate than if it were earned directly by you. So, whenever a spouse or child helps in the business, an opportunity exists to take advantage of valuable tax deductions.

Income Splitting - Spouse

Too often the spouse is not given a salary because the business simply can't afford it. Usually couples file a joint tax return with half the family income being taxed to each of them, no matter who earns it. But, adding a spouse to the payroll can add tax-sheltered dollars to the family bankroll. As an employee, the spouse can participate in a variety of tax-sheltered corporate benefits including pension and profit-sharing plans, group life insurance programs and company paid travel expenses.

✔ Pension and Profit-Sharing Plans
Entities filing an 1120 get a full deduction for its contribution to a husband and wife each year and the contributions are not taxable income until the spouse cashes in on the fund. Upon retirement, these funds receive favorable tax treatment from the IRS.

✔ Group Life Insurance
"C" Corporations and LLC's filing an 1120 tax election can purchase life insurance for its employees, including a husband and wife with the cost for premiums being deductible. Premiums covering the first $50,000 of insurance are not considered income either.

✔ Company Paid Travel Expenses
While it is difficult to deduct the travel expenses incurred by a spouse on business trips or conventions, if the spouse is an employee it is easier to show a legitimate business purpose for the trip. At that point, the spouse's expenses are deductible.

Income Splitting - Children

Children are often co-owners of small, family-oriented corporations and can be involved in a variety of odd jobs for the business. It may make sense to formally hire a child in those circumstances and pay them reasonable wages for the work they perform. Naturally, it is very important that everything is completely businesslike when a children works for a "C"

Corporation or an LLC filing an 1120 tax election. If the wages are not reasonable, or the work is not actually performed, your children may owe taxes on their earnings and the corporation could lose its deduction. But beyond the tax-sheltered benefits outlined for a spouse, employed children can use the full standard deduction to shield their income from taxes on the first $4,400 of earned income.

No matter how much your child is paid, you can still claim him or her as a dependency deduction on your individual income tax return (although the child cannot claim a personal exemption on his or her own return if he or she is claimed as a dependent on your return). The IRS determines that your child is still your dependent as long as you provide more than half the child's support and he or she either (won't reach the age of 19 this year, or is between the ages of 18 and 24 and a full time student during any five calendar months of the year).

The only way you can lose your deduction is if the child spends enough on his or her own support that at least half of it is self-provided. To avoid this, make sure the child puts enough of his or her earnings in the bank so that you can meet the criteria for providing at least half support. One of the negatives to this strategy for entities filing an 1120 is that Social Security, unemployment taxes and other state taxes that may apply must be paid for all employees regardless of their age. These taxes can swallow a significant percentage of worker's wages.

Independent Contractors

Persons who are not treated as employees for employment tax purposes.

Mean Testing

'Mean Testing' (penalizing the rich) is a growing trend and most often measured by the adjusted gross income (AGI) on a 1040. People over certain tax thresholds lose tax breaks and have to pay more taxes and penalties than do others. Income from an "S" Corporation or an LLC (filing a 1065) can make things even worse. Income on entities filing an 1120 tax election are not counted in most mean testing models.

Medical Expenses

Using a Medical Reimbursement Plan (MRP) under *[IRC § Section 105(b)]*, entities filing an 1120 can pay all medical expenses in pre-tax dollars. These expenses are 100% deductible to "C" Corporations and LLC's filing an 1120 and are not considered as income to the person receiving the benefits. Individuals, however, can only deduct medical expenses to the extent that they exceed 7.5% of their adjusted gross income (AGI). That means an individual with $50,000 of adjusted gross income cannot deduct the first $3,750 of their medical expenses, while a corporation can deduct it all.

Passive Income

Income to certain taxpayers (including Subchapter S- corporation shareholders) that is subject to the passive activity loss (PAL) rules because the taxpayer does not materially participate in the business activity producing the income. Generally includes receipts from royalties, rents, dividends, interest, annuities, and the sale and exchange of stock and securities.

Per Diem Benefits

Per Diem Benefits are a method of paying a flat reimbursement amount for certain expenditures, as opposed to choosing to paying itemized reimbursable expenses, both are non-taxable income and fully deductible. IRS Publication 463 *(previously IRS Publication 1542)* details the allowable payment for meals and lodging while traveling away from the office for business reasons. Such meals and lodging can be deducted 100% at the state level and by the IRS so long as the expense is an 'ordinary and necessary' business expense, whereas in-town business meals are deductible at a rate of only 50%. Or, if the expenses exceed the allowable amount for a city or state, the traveler can take the deduction using the receipts instead of the allowance set by the Internal Revenue Service.

Generally, entity approved per diems offer a rate of $40.00 per day which has proven to be acceptable for the owners or authorized employee (not independent contractors) who work past 6 pm on weekdays, over four hours on a weekend while working on company premises, or when traveling more than 20 miles from the company office.

Pre-Tax vs. After-Tax

The taxability of the individual is based on the gross (pre-tax) amount of the individual's income. Individuals receive income, pay taxes and ***then*** make purchases (or pay bills) with any remaining 'after-tax' money. The taxability of entities filing an 1120 tax election is based on the net (after tax) amount of income of the "C" Corporation or LLC filing an 1120. Entities filing an 1120 tax election receive income, buy things (or pay bills) and ***then*** pay taxes on any money remaining!

Profits and Losses

The profits and losses of a "C" Corporation, or LLC filing an 1120, are not passed through to the shareholders or members, but rather are taxed separately on an 1120 IRS tax form, thus entities filing an 1120 tax election are not a favored entity for people who need to produce tax losses to offset W-2 or 1099 type wages. However, if you are not in need of deducting such losses, "C" Corporations, or LLC's filing an 1120), can provide more verifiable deductions than any other type of entity (or tax election). Entities filing an 1120 tax election are required to file annual tax returns even if they earn no money during the year.

"C" Corporations, or LLC's filing an 1120, pay their own taxes usually at a lower rate than individual income tax rates. For example, the current tax rate for an 1120 is 15% of the first $50,000 of taxable income versus the individual rate of 28% of taxable income. As income rises, the corporate rate continues to be lower than the personal tax rate. Entities filing an 1120 tax election pay around 22.25% on the first $100,000 and less than 31% on the first $200,000. Individual can pay as much as 39% of $200,000 in taxable income.

With current 'progressive' tax rate structures, it is expensive to have too much income on any one tax return. For individuals, the nominal rates go from 10% to 15%, 25%, 28%, 33% and 35% with effective rates being even higher due to the phasing out of previous tax breaks as income increases. Individuals can pay as much as 39% of $200,000 in taxable income, again, without the ability to deduct most business expenses. If your corporate tax rate is 28% or more, you can keep up to $50,000 in profit to be taxed at 15%, then distribute the remaining after-tax net as a "qualified corporate dividend" to be taxed at 15%. This yields an effective tax rate of just 27.75% on $200,000 of taxable income, instead of 39%.

Rules of Attribution

The Internal Revenue Service (IRS) places restrictions how many "C" corporations a person may own and prohibits a person from creatively owning 50% of the stock in two or more "C" corporations simultaneously. From a tax perspective, multiple "C" corporations may be subject to filing a single tax return if the owner is in violation of the rules of attribution. The IRS rules of attribution consider a "C" corporation to be "one person" if 50% or more of the stock is held by you and your father, mother, brother(s), sister(s), husband, wife, son(s) or daughter(s). The same rules of attribution are applicable to the proper formation of a 'multi-member' Limited Liability Company wishing to file an 1120 tax election.

Salaries

Directors generally are not paid anything for being a director, except their expenses when attending directors meetings, whereas officers are considered employees of the corporation. As employees, officers (president, secretary, treasurer) should be paid a 'reasonable' salary for their services. Naturally, this salary would be personally taxable income to the recipient.

For entities filing an 1120 tax election, it would be unreasonable to pay officers a large salary, since all resources would be needed for start-up and cash flow expenses. Therefore, the Board of Directors can pass a resolution that "for the time being," officers shall forego their normal compensation until the "C" Corporation or LLC filing an 1120 is established and enjoys a solid cash flow. Meanwhile, you can take full advantage of all the tax-free benefits and pre-tax expenditures available from an entity filing an 1120.

Such a resolution would protect officers in another way too. Once the "C" Corporation or LLC filing an 1120 becomes profitable, it will probably be necessary for its officers to draw a larger salary. The board can then pass another resolution, stating that the entity is profitable and time to pay salaries commensurate to the responsibilities of its officers. These measures will protect you from attempts by the IRS to argue your salary is a disguised dividend and subject to extra taxes. Here is a sound rule of thumb for entities filing an 1120 tax election, *"expenses are to be paid first and then, if funds permit, salaries can be paid"*.

Once your "C" Corporation or LLC filing an 1120 has been running for several years, your compensation should be seen as reasonable in comparison to current market prices. It should be in the range that would be paid for 'like services' by 'like enterprises'. Happily, this gives you considerable leeway, as there is usually a large range of compensation executives receive within an industry.

Tax Deductions

The Internal Revenue Code (IRC) Section 179 expensing election is far more lucrative for owners of entities filing an 1120 because they can multiply their total deductions by splitting the purchases of business assets among differing business entities. Plus, the deduction for net rental losses is magnified by using a "C" Corporation, or LLC's filing an 1120, because they can use rental losses to offset operating income. With an "S" Corp or an LLC (filing a 1065), Section 179 deductions are limited to just one amount and rental losses are subject to the 25% restrictive passive loss rules.

Tax Return Filings

Unless an entity is exempt under Section 501 of the Internal Revenue Code, all domestic "C" Corporations or LLC's filing an 1120 (including any such entities in bankruptcy) must file an income tax return whether or not they have taxable income. Generally, the filing an income tax return is due by the 15th day of March after the end of its tax year as determined by the month stated on the entity's application for an EIN with the IRS; either a fiscal or calendar year.

Tax Return Filing Extensions

IRS Form 7004 requests a 6-month extension of time to file an 1120 income tax return. The Internal Revenue Services generally grants the extension automatically if you complete the form properly, file it, and pay any taxes that should be due by the due date for the return for which the extension applies.

Tax Flow-Chart
Entities Filing an 1120 Stand-Alone 'Corporate' Tax Election

GROSS INCOME

Gross Profit:

- Gross Sales
- Gross Receipts from Services, less
- Cost of Goods Sold

Includes 100% of Dividends in Gross Income, Interest, Rents and Royalties

Net Gain on Sales and Exchanges

Any other Income

Minus

DEDUCTIONS from Gross Income

Deductions:

Compensation of Officers

Salaries and Wages

Business Perks

Repairs, Bad Debts, Rents, Taxes, Interest

Ordinary Losses on Sales or Exchanges

Contributions, Advertising

Amortization, Depreciation and Depletion

Pension and Profit Sharing Plans; Employee Benefit Programs

Other, Including Casualty, Theft Losses, Research, Experimental Costs

And
Minus

SPECIAL Deductions

Special Deductions:

Manufacturer's Deduction

Net Operating Loss Deduction

Dividends-Received Deduction

Organizational Expense Amortization, Elective

Equals

TAXABLE INCOME

Taxable Income:

To which rates are applied

And from total tax there are deducted estimated tax payments for the year and if applicable, the Foreign Tax Credit, the Credit for Federal Excise Tax on Gasoline and Special Fuels and the Combined General Business Credit. And there is added any tax from re-computing a Prior Year's Investment Credit and any Alternative minimum Tax on Tax Preferences.

1120-S Tax Elections

Taxation for Entities Filing an 1120-S Tax Election Including "S" Corporations

An "S" Corporation (which files an 1120-S tax return), has a blend of characteristics that are associated with "C" Corporations (that file and 1120 tax return) and Limited Partnerships (that file a 1065 tax return). An "S" Corporation begins as a "C" Corporation and 'becomes' an "S" Corporation with the filing of IRS Form 8832. These changes allows the "S" Corporation to be taxed either like a sole proprietorship or partnership instead of a separate (stand alone) entity. "S" Corporations are corporations that elect not to pay tax themselves, but pass income and expenses directly through to their shareholders.

"S" Corporation Qualifications

To qualify as an "S" Corporation, a business must previously exist as a "C" Corporation and must be formed in the United States. "S" Corporations may issue only one class of stock and the shareholders may ***only*** consist of individuals who are U.S citizens (not 'green card' holders or non-resident aliens), estates, or certain types of qualifying trusts. However, "S" Corporations can own taxable or 'qualified subchapter S' subsidiaries *[IRC §1362(a)]*. The maximum number of shareholders in an "S" Corporation is limited to 100.

"S" Corporation Advantages

✔ Avoid Self-Employment Tax

Shareholders (who are also employees) draw salaries reported on Form W-2 and are subject to FICA tax. The corporate profits are passed through to their personal returns on a K-1 and taxed as ordinary income, but not subject to FICA or self-employment tax *[Rev. Rul. 59-221]*. You still have to pay yourself a reasonable salary *[IRC § 3101(a)]* otherwise the IRS can recharacterize your dividend as wages and impose employment tax *[IRC § 3121(d)(1), 4Radtke v. Comm'r, 895 F.2d 1196 (7th Cir. 1996)]*. "Reasonable compensation" varies from industry to industry, so be sure you can justify the salary you choose *[IRC § 6651]*.

✔ Offset Income

"S" Corporation losses can be used up to your "basis" in the business to offset outside income from salaries, investments and other businesses. Basis has been determined to include cash and stock contributed to the corporation and loans made to the corporation, but ***not*** loans personally guaranteed on behalf of the corporation. If you finance a startup in which you reasonably expect to lose money initially, consider using an LLC to boost deductible losses.

✔ Shift Income

An "S" Corporation can be used to shift income to lower-bracket shareholders. Shares in the corporation may go to children or other lower-bracket beneficiaries so that their share of profits is taxed at their lower rate.

✔ Take Losses

An "S" Corporation, like a partnership or an LLC (filing a 1065), avoids the problem of double taxation on its earnings. Instead, profits and losses 'pass-through' the corporation and are reported by the shareholders on their individual tax returns. "S" Corporations are similar in many ways to an LLC (filing a 1065) in that losses can be past onto an individual's 1040 tax return to help 'offset' W-2 or 1099 wages. If losses exceed income they generate net operating losses ("NOLs") that can carry back two years or forward 20 years.

"S" Corporation Disadvantages

✖ Additional Taxes

Some states impose special taxes on the pass-through income of "S" Corporations. For example, in addition to California's $800 annual franchise fees, the state of California imposes an additional 1.5% tax on "S" Corporations. Be sure to include such taxes in your planning.

❌ Limit Qualified Plans

"S" Corporations limited qualified plans and IRA contributions based on the percentage of income. Consider SIMPLE IRA's, 401(k), or defined benefit plans for contributions not strictly limited to a percentage of salary income *[6Durando v. U.S., 70 F.3d 548 (9th Cir. 1995)]*.

❌ Phantom Income

With an "S" Corporation (or an LLC filing a 1065), the corporate shareholders, or LLC members, are required to pay income tax on their share of the entity's income regardless of whether they take any money out of the entity's account. Entities filing an 1120 tax election can accumulate earnings and pay tax at the corporate level without the shareholders or members being individually taxed. Were "S" Corporations or LLC's (filing a 1065) to attempt to accumulate earnings, the shareholders or members could be subject to "Phantom Income" and therefore be taxed on income not actually earned.

For example, if a person had $250,000 of "S" Corporation income on his or her 1040 but had only taken out $25,000 they could be liable to pay more income tax than actual income received. This type of taxability is called 'phantom income'. Adding insult to injury, if a person had child support arrangements requiring the payment of 30% of their adjusted gross income (AGI) each year, they could be liable to pay 30% on the full amount of $250,000 to an ex-spouse. Opting for a "C" Corporation, or an LLC filing an 1120, instead of an "S" Corporation or an LLC (filing a 1065) could have shifted all or part of this income to the corporation and their taxable income and excess child support liabilities could be significantly reduced. It would be better if the corporation lost money because this loss would be applied to the shareholder's 1040 tax return, thus offering them tax relief instead of tax anguish.

❌ Gains

The pass-through feature of passing on losses *can* be positive *if* you have losses to offset, but if you are passing on profits you could be paying the maximum amount possible in taxes!

❌ Under IRS Attack

The IRS has been increasing its attacks on "S" Corporations because of its 'flow-through' status. Shareholders who also perform services for "S" Corporations may divide their income from the corporation into two categories of salary and dividends. Salary is subject to Medicare and FICA withholdings. Since dividends are taxed at a higher rate when included in the shareholder's 1040 tax returns, shareholders want to take as much of the income as salary as possible while the IRS wants to see more dividends being paid to the shareholders.

1065 Tax Elections

**Taxation for Entities Filing a 1065 Tax Election
Including 'Multi-Member' Limited Liability Companies and Limited Partnerships**

Since LLC's (filing a 1065) and Limited Partnerships are 'pass-through' entities, there is no potential for income to be taxed on the 'entity level'. Unlike Corporations (and irrevocable trusts), entities filing a 1065 tax election are not taxpaying entities. LLC's (filing a 1065) and LP's submit an annual informational tax return setting forth their income and expenses, but do not pay tax on their net income. Instead, the proportionate amount of income or loss for each member or partner is passed-through from the company or partnership to the individual. Each member or partner claims his or her respective deductions and income or loss on his or her own tax return.

Entities filing a 1065 tax election are regularly used for real estate investors and tax shelter investments in order to pass tax deductions and income or loss through to the individual investors. Losses are often used by members and partners to offset other income they might have from other sources. Although LLC's (filing an 1065) and LP's are entities which do not pay tax themselves, they must never-the-less report their expenses and income or losses so their respective members or partners may account for their portion of the deductions and income or loss on their personal income tax returns.

Any income or deductions not separated among the various members or partners are combined and reported into the overall taxable income or loss of the company or partnership. All income and expense items for entities filing a 1065, including information regarding deductions and ordinary income or loss, are reported on a Schedule K. The deductions and credit or loss items are then allocated to each member or partner on a Schedule K-1 and furnished to the respective member or partner.

Saving Income and Estate Taxes

If family assets are held in the form of an LLC (filing a 1065) or an LP, it is possible to obtain certain income and estate tax savings in addition to asset protection benefits. Income tax savings can be realized by spreading income from high tax bracket parents to lower tax brackets of children and/or grandchildren who are fourteen years or older. Estate tax reductions can be accomplished because of certain unique attributes of entities filing a 1065, which are not present in any other type of tax election. Gifting membership or partnership interests to your children or other family members can reduce the overall size of your estate and potential estate tax liabilities while maintaining the important ability to shift the value of assets out of your estate without any loss of control.

Self Employment and Withholding Tax

If an individual acts as the managing member of an LLC (filing a 1065) or the general partner of an LP, all income passed through shall be subject to self-employment taxes which are 15.3%. However if the managing member or general partner is a "C" Corporation, there is no such self-employment tax liability. Employees of an LLC (filing a 1065) or a LP are subject to withholding taxes where W-2 or 1099 forms are required to be filed.

Liabilities and debts for members of an LLC (fling a 1065) or limited partners of a LP are limited by State law. However general partners of a Limited Partnership may be held personally liable in situations involving unpaid employee withholdings. State laws vary and each State may determine the extent to which a general partner of a Limited Partnership is liable for the partnership obligations, including federal tax liabilities. See:

> *United States v. Papandon, 331 F.3d 52, 55-56 (2d Cir. 2003)*
> *Remington v. United States, 210 F.3d 281, 283 (5th Cir. 2000)*
> *United States v. Galletti, 72 U.S.L.W. 4252 (U.S. March 23, 2004)*

In contrast, members of a Limited Liability Company are generally not liable under State law for the debts of an LLC. See:

> *N.Y. Ltd. Liab. Co. Law § 609(a) (McKinney Supp. 2003)*

If under state law the members of an LLC (filing a 1065) are not liable for the tax debts of the LLC, then absent fraudulent transfers or other special circumstances, the IRS may not collect the LLC's employment tax liability from the members, including by levy on the property and rights to property of the members. See:

Scott v. Commissioner, 236 F.3d 1239 (10th Cir. 2001)
Stanko v. Commissioner, 209 F.3d 1082 (8th Cir. 2000)

Although, depending on the facts of the case regarding fraudulent transfers or other special circumstances, a member may be liable for a trust fund recovery penalty under I.R.C. § 6672.

Tax Flow-Chart
Entities Filing a 1065 Flow-Thru 'Partnership' Tax Election

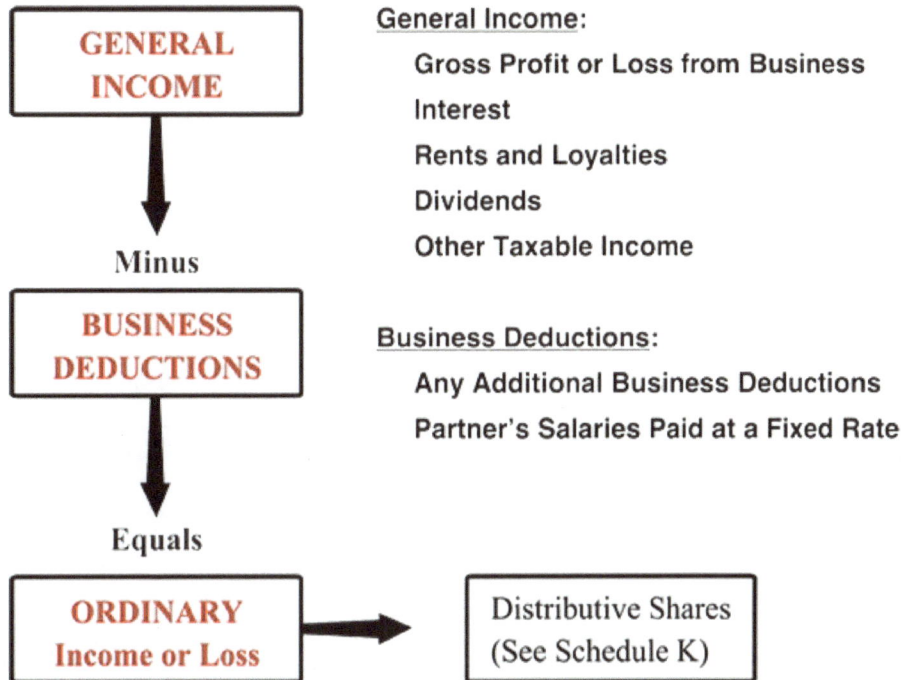

GENERAL INCOME

Minus

BUSINESS DEDUCTIONS

Equals

ORDINARY Income or Loss → Distributive Shares (See Schedule K)

General Income:
  Gross Profit or Loss from Business
  Interest
  Rents and Loyalties
  Dividends
  Other Taxable Income

Business Deductions:
  Any Additional Business Deductions
  Partner's Salaries Paid at a Fixed Rate

California Tax Strategies

California Taxation for Limited Liability Companies (LLC)

The Beverly-Killea Limited Liability Company Act of 1994 authorized the formation of 'domestic' LLC's formed in California and recognized out-of-state LLC's (known as a 'foreign' entity) and out-of-country LLC's (known as an 'alien' entity) to conduct business in California.

A Limited Liability Company's tax classification (whether a 'single-member' company and disregarded as an entity for tax purposes, a 'multi-member' entity taxed as a partnership on a 1065, or 'multi-member' entity taxed as a "C" Corporation on an 1120) generally determines the member's California income, deductions and credits under personal income tax law. Members of an LLC classified as an 1120 for tax purposes generally determine their California income under corporate tax law. But members of an LLC (filing a 1065) or partners of an LP conducting business in any state outside California, wherein the members or partners 'reside' in California, shall be taxed as though they were doing business in California.

Annual California Fees

California has an annual $800 pre-paid tax for the privilege of conducting business in California, regardless of whether any business is actually conducted or not, unless the LLC conducted no business in California and the taxable year was 15 days or less. This annual tax is due for all California Limited Liability Companies whether domestic, foreign or alien.

✅ Domestic LLC

For domestic California LLC's, this tax is due on the 15th day of the fourth month after the beginning of the taxable year.

✅ Foreign or Alien LLC

For LLC's foreign or alien LLC's registering to conducting business in the State of California, this tax is due immediately upon commencing business in California or registering with the California Secretary of State.

✅ Single-Member LLC

And, even though California legislation permits an LLC with a single-member to be disregarded for most tax purposes, single-member Limited Liability Companies in California are also subject to the said annual $800 California tax.

✅ Every California LLC

Every LLC conducting business in the State of California must file a Limited Liability Company tax voucher (FTB 3522) with the California Franchise Tax Board to pay the annual tax.

California LLC's Filing a 1065 Tax Election

A California LLC that has elected to file a 1065 tax election, and be treated as a partnership for tax purposes, uses a Schedule K-1 (Form 568) to report individual members' share of the LLC's income, deductions and credits, etc. The State of California will only accept a California Schedule K-1 by means of California Form 568 in a paperless format or via CD, diskette or cartridge.

Conducting Intrastate Business

The California Corporations Code outlines under what conditions or circumstance a foreign or alien Limited Liability Company is 'conducting intrastate business' within the State of California:

California Corporations Code
(Limited Liability Companies) Section 17001

(ap) *"Transact intrastate business" means to enter into repeated and successive transactions of business in this state, other than in interstate or foreign commerce.*

(1) *Without excluding other activities which may not be considered to be transacting intrastate business, a foreign limited liability company shall not be considered to be transacting intrastate business merely because its subsidiary transacts intrastate business, or merely because of its status as any one or more of the following:*

(A) A shareholder of a domestic corporation.

(B) A shareholder of a foreign corporation transacting intrastate business.

(C) A limited partner of a foreign limited partnership transacting intrastate business.

(D) A limited partner of a domestic limited partnership.

(E) A member or manager of a foreign limited liability company transacting intrastate business.

(F) A member or manager of a domestic limited liability company.

(2) Without excluding other activities which may not be considered to be transacting intrastate business, a foreign limited liability company shall not be considered to be transacting intrastate business within the meaning of this subdivision solely by reason of carrying on in this state any one or more of the following activities:

(A) Maintaining or defending any action or suit or any administrative or arbitration proceeding, or effecting the settlement thereof, or the settlement of claims or disputes.

(B) Holding meetings of its managers or members or carrying on any other activities concerning its internal affairs.

(C) Maintaining bank accounts.

(D) Maintaining offices or agencies for the transfer, exchange, and registration of the foreign limited liability company's securities or maintaining trustees or depositaries with respect to those securities.

(E) Effecting sales through independent contractors.

(F) Soliciting or procuring orders, whether by mail or through employees or agents or otherwise, where those orders require acceptance without this state before becoming binding contracts.

(G) Creating or acquiring evidences of debt or mortgages, liens, or security interests in real or personal property.

(H) Securing or collecting debts or enforcing mortgages and security interests in property securing the debts.

(I) Conducting an isolated transaction that is completed within 180 days and not in the course of a number of repeated transactions of a like nature.

Filing Extensions

If a California LLC files the Franchise Tax Board Form (FTB 3537), the State of California will grant an automatic six (6) month extension of time to file a return. The automatic extension will apply if the tax return is filed by the 15th day of the tenth month following the close of the taxable year. But an extension of time to file is not an extension of time to pay. You must pay the full balance by the original due date of the return (the 15th day of the fourth month following the close of the taxable year) to avoid penalties and interest.

Graduated Tax

The California Revenue and Taxation Code Section 17942(a) imposes a fee in addition to the minimum franchise tax, as determined by an entity's 'total income' or gross revenues. Under this Section, the amount of the fee is determined as follows:

Gross Revenue	Graduated Tax
$ 250,000	$ 900
$ 500,000	$ 2,500
$ 1,000,000	$ 6,000
$ 5,000,000 +	$ 11,790

Overall, the amount of the fee is relatively small, but is assessed against gross revenues, notwithstanding profitability. For example:

at $ 250,000 in gross revenues the fee is 0.36% of revenues;
at $ 500,000 in gross revenues the fee is 0.50% of revenues;
at $1,000,000 in gross revenues the fee is 0.60% of revenues;
at $5,000,000 in gross revenues the fee is 0.24% of revenues.

Refusal to Sign

If a non-resident member of an LLC (filing a 1065) conducting business in the State of California refuses to sign the Limited Liability Company Non-Resident Members Consent Form (FTB 3832), the LLC must compute and pay the members tax liability with Form 568, Side 2. (See: Instructions for Schedule T, Non-Consenting Non-Resident Members Tax Liability).

Return of Income

LLC's conducting business in California shall use Form 568 which is a 'Return of Income' to report their income and pan any non-consenting non-resident member tax by the 15th day of the fourth month following the close of its taxable year.

Worldwide Gross Income Tax

California Limited Liability Companies conducting business in the State of California are subject to an annual fee based on their total income. 'Total income' is defined as the sum of an LLC's 'worldwide gross income plus the cost of goods sold' according to the California Revenue and Taxation Code Section 24271.

California
Limited Liability Company vs. Limited Partnership

Appointment of Officers

California law provides for the appointment of officers in a Limited Liability Company (LLC). This can be useful when obtaining "directors and officers" insurance coverage for the principals in a company. There is no similar provision in California partnership law, making it more difficult to obtain insurance for the management of Limited Partnerships (LP).

Avoidance of California Property Reassessment Tax

California Proposition13 essentially disallows annual increases of more than 2% in the assessed value of California real property for property tax purposes, unless there is a change in ownership of such property. The effect of Proposition 13 is that property owners can continue to pay property taxes based on relatively low assessed values. A change in ownership of property can cause reassessment, but California law does provide that certain types of transfers are exempt from such reassessment. Reassessment occurs when more than 50% of the partnership interests are transferred. By structuring an (Family) Limited Partnership (FLP) properly a reassessment of real property, for California property tax purposes, can be avoided.

For example, let us assume that husband and wife own a piece of land out-right (no liens or debts) which they contribute a FLP in exchange for a100% interest in the FLP. The transaction does not trigger a reassessment of the property; it is merely a change in the form of ownership because husband's and wife's percentage ownership in the property prior to and after the transaction are identical. (If the couple has a bank loan against the property, they could first place the home into a Land Trust, for the avoidance of a due-on-sale under the Garn-St Germain Act, and make the beneficial interest holder the Limited Partnership.)

However, if the husband and wife then transfer more than 50% of their interest in the partnership to any third-party, the entire property will be reassessed to its current value for property tax purposes. To avoid the California reassessment tax, when a husband and wife want to pass their assets to their children, it can be accomplished by structuring the transaction so that the husband and wife first transfer more than 50% of their interest (say 52%) in the property to their son(s) and/or daughter(s). (In California, under Proposition 13, transfers of property between parents and children are exempt from reassessment taxes).

The husband and wife and their son(s) and/or daughter(s) can then contribute their respective interests in the property to the FLP (in exchange for proportional interests in the FLP). In this case, the husband and wife would receive a 48% interest in the FLP and their daughter would receive a 52% interest.

Because all partners own the exact percentage interest in the property both before and after the contributions, such transaction is exempt from reassessment in California. Further, The husband and wife can transfer up to their entire 48% FLP interest to their son(s) and/or daughter(s), without triggering a reassessment of the property owned by the FLP, because no more than 50% of the FLP will have changed hands in this scenario.

Discounted Value for Estate Tax and Gift Tax

California partnership law places certain restrictions on the transfer of voting rights to persons or entities that are not partners. Such restrictions result in the owner of a limited partnership interest having less control over the assets held in the Limited Partnership than if such owner held the assets outright. These restrictions mean that the owner of a limited partnership interest usually cannot sell its Limited Partnership interest as quickly or easily as selling an interest in the underlying assets. For this reason, the value of a limited partnership interest is generally lower than the pro-rata value of the underlying assets owned by the Limited Partnership. In the past, the IRS has accepted discounts in value of between 15% and 50% for limited partnership interests

Detriments to Forming a California Limited Partnership

1. A California Limited Partnership, being an entity with a separate legal personality, will have to pay the relatively-high annual $800 fee, maintain separate records and file a separate 1065 tax return.

2. California Limited Partnerships may be subject to the minimum franchise tax if the gross amount of transactions reach or exceeds $250,000 in one year, even if the assets in the California Limited Partnership earn no income.

3. If a California (Family) Limited Partnership is incorrectly formed and/or transfers the interests (as described above in the 'Avoidance of California Property Reassessment Tax') incorrectly, the transaction could trigger a reassessment of property values for California property tax purposes.

Strategies for California Businesses

Having entities in your home state can create a loss of income from 3% to 12% to corporate taxes. If you have an entity qualified within the state of California, and are using California as your entity base, you are paying a minimum of $9,600 in taxes on every $100,000 of taxable income. Many clients have solved this problem by moving their entity base, or setting up an additional entity to provide services in Nevada or Wyoming.

Business owners often personally provide the capital and services needed for their operations. But with a little more imagination, a Nevada or Wyoming based entity could be utilized to provide those very same functions. As every business needs to be properly managed, your Nevada or Wyoming entity could be in the business of licensing, consulting, advertising, or even sales and marketing, then contract with your present entity to provide such management related services.

Strategy 1

If a California business, after related deductions, has a taxable income of say $200,000 in the course of a year, that amounts to roughly $19,200 in state taxes. Were a Nevada or Wyoming entity properly invoiced for licensing fees in the amount of $150,000, such management fees are tax deductible and could reduce the total home state taxable income to only $50,000. By providing additional legitimate accounting, consulting, or sales and marketing services to your current entity at a fee-based cost of $45,000, it would leave only $5,000 in taxable California income.

If you have appointed nominee officers, directors, partners or members to your Nevada or Wyoming entity, there is no connection whatsoever to the ownership of the Nevada or Wyoming entity (which is not public knowledge) and that of the existing entity in your home state (which most likely discloses ownership). Nevada and Wyoming have no corporate income tax and no personal income tax, and any income which leave your home state entity and appears in your Nevada or Wyoming business entity may save you thousands of dollars in home state taxes.

This strategy provides you with a completely legal means of paying the least amount of tax on the money you have worked so hard to earn. Even if you're a home based business in a state which has high state income tax, but your distributors are located in many states, then this strategy reduces your home state income by the amount generated in those other jurisdictions. Such strategies for using a Nevada or Wyoming entity to your advantage can also include eliminating state capital gains tax, state sales tax, and escrow fees on the sale of real estate.

Strategy 2

Tax liens can be very stressful and, if not addressed prior to the notification of such a lien, can be problematic at best to remove. Consider forming a Nevada or Wyoming entity to which your present business is eternally indebted through the proper filing of a UCC-1 form in the applicable jurisdiction wherein your home state business is located.

Such a Nevada or Wyoming entity, that has the 'first position lien' on all of the assets in your current business, is considered *"First in Time; First in Line."* Should a tax court win a judgment (that may have otherwise closed down the business in your home state), the Nevada or Wyoming entity holds a prior lien and takes possession of the assets to which it has a legal right. Because you have acted legally (and chosen the state of Nevada or Wyoming in which to incorporate), under the 5th Amendment to the U.S. Constitution you are under no obligation to disclose ownership of the Nevada or Wyoming entity.

Strategy 3

An employee filing a 1040 federal income tax return only qualifies for four primary tax deductions; home, children, rental properties and limited business deductions. If such an employee making $100,000 for the year lived in California, the taxes on those earnings will be exorbitantly high and may be subject to 9.3% in personal income tax, 6.3% in social security, 1.45% in medicare tax, and 28% in federal taxes with a total tax exposure of 45% or $45,000 in earnings.

If the employee had a home based business, or if the employer was willing (and able) to hire a California "C" corporation, the now independent contractor would stand to qualify for hundreds of tax deductions and could re-characterize the income as W-2 earnings from the California "C" corporation could be as little as 50% of the original earnings. The remaining $50,000 could be expensed to a Nevada or Wyoming entity in the form of a licensing agreement fee (avoiding the 8.4% California corporate tax) and the balance could be left in the Nevada or Wyoming entity as retained earnings or expensed through legitimate tax deductible items and medical expense deductions. Thus, the tax consequences would be a maximum of $22,500 on the personal income and 15% (or $7,500) on the corporate income for a total of $30,000 in taxes. This example alone would save a minimum of $15,000 on this person's taxable income each and every year.

Federal and State Income Taxes

Intended Purpose

The following list of federal and state income taxes may not be current, but need not be current for its intended purpose. This illustration is designed to show the disparity between corporate and individual income taxes among the respective states. As with any tax advice, please seek competent counsel in your home jurisdiction.

Federal "Corporate" Income Tax for Entities Filing an 1120

$ 0	to	$ 50,000	15%	
$ 50,000	to	$ 75,000	$ 7,500 + 25% of the amount over	$ 50,000
$ 75,000	to	$ 100,000	$ 13,750 + 34% of the amount over	$ 75,000
$ 100,000	to	$ 335,000	$ 22,250 + 39% of the amount over	$ 100,000
$ 335,000	to	$ 10,000,000	$ 113,900 + 34% of the amount over	$ 335,000
$ 10,000,000	to	$ 15,000,000	$ 3,400,000 + 35% of the amount over	$ 10,000,000
$ 15,000,000	to	$ 18,333,333	$ 5,150,000 + 38% of the amount over	$ 15,000,000
$ 18,333,333	to	$ and up	35%	

Federal Income Tax for Individuals (Single) Filing a 1040

$ 0	to	$ 8,925	10%
$ 8,926	to	$ 36,250	15%
$ 36,251	to	$ 87,850	25%
$ 87,851	to	$ 183,250	28%
$ 183,251	to	$ 398,350	33%
$ 398,351	to	$ 400,000	35%
$ 400,001	to	$ and up	39.6%

State Income Tax

State	Corporate Income Tax		Individual Income Tax (Single)	
Alabama	6.5%	> $0	2.0% 4.0% 5.0%	> $0 > $500 > $3,000
Alaska	1.0% 2.0% 3.0% 4.0% 5.0% 6.0% 7.0% 8.0% 9.0% 9.4%	> $0 > $10,000 > $20,000 > $30,000 > $40,000 > $50,000 > $60,000 > $70,000 > $80,000 > $90,000	*No Personal Income Tax*	
Arizona	6.5%	> $0 *(Minimum $50)*	2.59% 2.88% 3.36% 4.24% 4.54%	> $0 > $10,000 > $25,000 > $50,000 > $150,000
Arkansas	1.0% 2.0% 3.0% 5.0% 6.0% 6.5%	> $0 > $3,000 > $6,000 > $11,000 > $25,000 > $100,000	1.0% 2.5% 3.5% 4.5% 6.0% 7.0%	> $0 > $4,099 > $8,199 > $12,199 > $20,399 > $33,999
California	8.84% > $0 *(Minimum $800)* *Additional 1.50% for "S" Corp's* *Plus Graduated Taxes for LLC's*		1.0% 2.0% 4.0% 6.0% 8.0% 9.3% 10.3% 11.3% 12.3% 13.3%	> $0 > $7,455 > $17,676 > $27,897 > $38,726 > $48,942 > $250,000 > $300,000 > $500,000 > $1,000,000
Colorado	4.63%	> $0	4.63%	> $0

State	Corporate Income Tax		Individual Income Tax (Single)	
Connecticut	9.0%	> $0	3.0%	> $0
			5.0%	> $10,000
			5.5%	> $50,000
			6.0%	> $100,000
			6.5%	> $200,000
			6.7%	> $250,000
Delaware	8.7%	> $0	2.2%	> $2,000
	(Plus Gross Receipts Tax)		3.90%	> $5,000
			4.80%	> $10,000
			5.20%	> $20,000
			5.55%	> $25,000
			6.75%	> $60,000
District of Columbia	9.975%	> $0	4.0%	> $0
			6.0%	> $10,000
			8.5%	> $40,000
			8.95%	> $350,000
Florida	5.5%	> $0	*No Personal Income Tax*	
Georgia	6.0%	> $0	1.0%	> $0
			2.0%	> $750
			3.0%	> $2,250
			4.0%	> $3,750
			5.0%	> $5,250
			6.0%	> $7,000
Hawaii	4.4%	> $0	1.4%	> $0
	5.4%	> $25,000	3.2%	> $2,400
	6.4%	> $100,000	5.5%	> $4,800
			6.4%	> $9,600
			6.8%	> $14,400
			7.2%	> $19,200
			7.6%	> $24,000
			7.9%	> $36,000
			8.25%	> $48,000
			9.0%	> $150,000
			10.0%	> $175,000
			11.0%	> $200,000

State	Corporate Income Tax		Individual Income Tax (Single)	
Idaho	7.4%	> $0 *(Minimum $20)*	1.6%	> $0
			3.6%	> $1,380
			4.1%	> $2,760
			5.1%	> $4,140
			6.1%	> $5,520
			7.1%	> $6,900
			7.4%	> $10,350
Illinois	9.5%	> $0	5.0% of Federal Adjusted Gross Income	
Indiana	8.0%	> $0	3.4% of Federal Adjusted Gross Income	
Iowa	6.0%	> $0	0.36%	> $0
	8.0%	> $25,000	0.72%	> $1,494
	10.0%	> $100,000	2.43%	> $2,988
	12.0%	> $250,000	4.50%	> $5,976
			6.12%	> $13,446
			6.48%	> $22,410
			6.80%	> $29,880
			7.92%	> $44,820
			8.98%	> $67,230
Kansas	4.0%	> $0	3.0%	> $0
	7.0%	> $50,000	4.9%	> $15,000
Kentucky	4.0%	> $0	2.0%	> $0
	5.0%	> $50,000	3.0%	> $3,000
	6.0%	> $100,000	4.0%	> $4,000
			5.0%	> $5,000
			5.8%	> $8,000
			6.0%	> $75,000
Louisiana	4.0%	> $0	2.0%	> $0
	5.0%	> $25,000	4.0%	> $12,500
	6.0%	> $50,000	6.0%	> $50,000
	7.0%	> $100,000		
	8.0%	> $200,000		
Maine	3.50%	> $0	6.5%	> $5,200
	7.93%	> $25,000	7.95%	> $20,900
	8.33%	> $75,000		
	8.93%	> $250,000		

State	Corporate Income Tax		Individual Income Tax (Single)	
Maryland	8.25%	> $0	2.0%	> $0
			3.0%	> $1,000
			4.0%	> $2,000
			4.75%	> $3,000
			5.0%	> $100,000
			5.25%	> $125,000
			5.5%	> $150,000
			5.75%	> $250,000
Massachusetts	8.0%	> $0 *(Minimum $456)*	5.25%	> $0
Michigan	6.0%	> $0 *(Excludes Single Businesses)*	4.25% of Federal Adjusted Gross Income	
Minnesota	9.8%	> $0	5.35%	> $0
			7.05%	> $24,270
			7.85%	> $79,730
Mississippi	3.0%	> $0	3.0%	> $0
	4.0%	> $5,000	4.0%	> $5,000
	5.0%	> $10,000	5.0%	> $10,000
Missouri	6.25%	> $0	1.5%	> $0
			2.0%	> $1,000
			2.5%	> $2,000
			3.0%	> $3,000
			3.5%	> $4,000
			4.0%	> $5,000
			4.5%	> $6,000
			5.0%	> $7,000
			5.5%	> $8,000
			6.0%	> $9,000
Montana	6.75%	> $0 *(Minimum $50)*	1.0%	> $0
			2.0%	> $2,700
			3.0%	> $4,800
			4.0%	> $7,300
			5.0%	> $9,900
			6.0%	> $12.700
			6.9%	> $16,400
Nebraska	5.58%	> $0	2.46%	> $0
	7.81%	> $100,000	3.51%	> $2,400
			5.01%	> $17,500
			6.84%	> $27,000
Nevada	*No Corporate Income Tax*		*No Personal Income Tax*	

State	Corporate Income Tax		Individual Income Tax (Single)	
New Hampshire	8.5%	> $0	5%	> $0
New Jersey	9.0%	> $100,000	1.40%	> $0
	(Minimum $500)		1.75%	> $20,000
	Additional 1.33% for "S" Corp's		3.50%	> $35,000
			5.525%	> $40,000
			6.37%	> $75,000
			8.97%	> $500,000
New Mexico	4.8%	> $0	1.7%	> $0
	6.4%	> $500,000	3.2%	> $5,500
	7.6%	> $1,000,000	4.7%	> $11,000
			4.9%	> $16,000
New York	7.1%	> $0	4.00%	> $0
			4.50%	> $8,200
			5.25%	> $11,300
			5.90%	> $13,350
			6.45%	> $20,550
			6.65%	> $77,150
			6.85%	> $20,850
			8.82%	> $1,029,250
North Carolina	6.9%	> $0	6.00%	> $0
			7.00%	> $12,750
			7.75%	> $60,000
North Dakota	1.68%	> $0	1.51%	> $0
	4.23%	> $25,000	2.82%	> $36,250
	5.15%	> $50,000	3.13%	> $87,850
			3.63%	> $183,250
			3.99%	> $398,350
Ohio	No broad-based income tax		0.58%	> $0
	(Franchise Tax)		1.174%	> $5,200
			2.348%	> $10,400
			2.945%	> $15,560
			3.521%	> $20,900
			4.109%	> $41,700
			4.695%	> $83,350
			5.451%	> $104,250
			5.925%	> $208,500

State	Corporate Income Tax		Individual Income Tax (Single)	
Oklahoma	6.0%	> $0	0.5%	> $0
			1.0%	> $1,000
			2.0%	> $2,500
			3.0%	> $3,750
			4.0%	> $4,900
			5.0%	> $7,200
			5.25%	> $8,700
Oregon	6.6%	> $0 *(Minimum $10)*	5.0%	> $0
	7.6%	> $10,000,000	7.0%	> $3,250
			9.0%	> $8,150
			9.9%	> $125,000
Pennsylvania	9.99%	> $0	3.07%	> $0
Rhode Island	9.0%	> $0 *(Minimum $250)*	3.75%	> $0
			4.75%	> $58,600
			5.99%	> $133,250
South Carolina	5.0%	> $0	0%	> $0
			3.0%	> $2,850
			4.0%	> $5,700
			5.0%	> $8,550
			6.0%	> $11,400
			7.0%	> $14,250
South Dakota	No broad-based income tax *(Minimum $500)*		*No Personal Income Tax*	
Tennessee	6.5%	> $0	6.0%	> $0
Texas	No broad-based income tax *(Franchise Tax)*		*No Personal Income Tax*	
Utah	5.0%	> $0 *(Minimum $100)*	5.0%	> $0
Vermont	6.0%	> $0	3.55%	> $0
	7.0%	> $10,000	6.8%	> $36,250
	8.5%	> $25,000	7.8%	> $87,850
			8.8%	> $183,250
			8.95%	> $398,350
Virginia	6.0% *(Minimum $250)* *Plus Gross Receipts Tax*		2.0%	> $0
			3.0%	> $3,000
			5.0%	> $5,000
			5.75%	> $17,000

State	Corporate Income Tax	Individual Income Tax (Single)
Washington	No broad-based income tax (Franchise Tax)	*No Personal Income Tax*
West Virginia	7.0% > $0	3.0% > $0 4.0% > $10,000 4.5% > $25,000 6.0% > $40,000 6.5% > $60,000
Wisconsin	7.9% > $0	4.60% > $0 6.15% > $10,750 6.50% > $21,490 6.75% > $161,180 7.75% > $236,600
Wyoming	No broad-based income tax (Minimum $50)	*No Personal Income Tax*

What is a Trust?

What is a Trust?

"A trust is an equitable obligation, binding a person (trustee) to deal with property owned by him (trust property as opposed to private property) for the benefit of persons (beneficiaries)."

– Sir Arthur Underhill, 1945

A trust is a contractual relationship. Trusts have been used for hundreds of years. In fact, the first recorded trust in America was in the 1600's and was formed by the governor of the Virginia Colony. So, there are many types of trusts and many purposes for their creation.

Trusts are primarily created for the management and distribution of assets during a person's life or after their death. A trust may be created for a surviving spouse, children, friend, business, charitable organization or for the financial benefit of the person creating the trust. Trust law is voluminous, but generally a trust has been lawfully created if properly funded, if a disinterested third-party trustee has properly held and maintained the trust assets, and if the purpose of the trust is legitimate according to established trust law. A trust is comprised of four separate and distinct parts.

Trust

Settlor

Trustee

Beneficiary

Trust

Settlor

Often called a grantor, a settlor is the person who creates the trust. A settlor determines the terms and conditions whereupon assets are to be inherited or disbursed.

Trustee

The individual (or entity) who holds, manages and disburses the assets of the trust is called a trustee and has a fiduciary responsibility to act in good faith and administer the terms and conditions of the trust agreement in accordance with general trust law principles. Under general trust law principles, a trustee is a fiduciary for the beneficiaries. Black's Law dictionary defines a fiduciary as:

> *"One who stands not for his own benefit, but for the benefit of another person, as to whom he stands in a relation implying and necessitating great confidence and trust on the one part, and a high degree of good faith on the other part."*

The operative terms being 'great confidence' and 'high degree of good faith'. A trustee must act in a way that is well beyond what is expected of the average person. In the event a trustee is required to exercise judgment in carrying out trust duties, the trustee is be held to that higher standard.

Beneficiary

The person who is benefited by the trust is known as the beneficiary and may be an individual or multiple people, a corporation, limited liability company, limited partnership, living trust or any combination thereof. A beneficiary has rights to receive assets and profits from the trust and may be granted rights to retain management control of the trust. Beneficiaries are *not* considered 'partners' like partners in a general partnership. They cannot dissolve their arrangement with other beneficiaries and they cannot go to court to force the dissolution or an accounting of the trust arrangement, nor can beneficiaries 'bind' each other for trust obligations.

Trust

The trust is the formal written agreement and the assets that comprise the body of the trust *(corpus)*. A trust becomes active, or activated, once it has been funded with assets. Funding requires the transference of asset ownership from the settlor to the trust. Once this transfer of assets is complete, the settlor no longer has legal or equitable title of those assets.

Trust Basics

People often have a difficult time understanding trusts, mainly because they confuse the concept of a trust with that of a corporation. A corporation is a distinct legal entity that stands apart as a separate legal personality from its owners. *A trust is not an entity but rather a legal arrangement created by an agreement. Although a trust may be created under state law, it is not created by a state nor registered with the Secretary of State.* Again, a trust is an agreement (or contractual arrangement) by which one party (trustee or co-trustee) holds title to property for the benefit of another (the beneficiaries) in a fiduciary capacity.

A trust is created when a settlor executes a trust agreement with a trustee. The trust agreement states exactly how the trustee is to handle, manage and distribute trust assets for the benefit of its beneficiaries. Once the trust agreement has been established, the trust must be 'funded' with assets to be a completed agreement or arrangement.

Trust assets can consist of 'real property' (real estate) or 'personal property', which is tangible property other than real estate such as money, stocks or bonds and even includes titled assets other than real estate. The rights and conveniences of ownership are exercised by the beneficial owner (the beneficiaries), whose interests are generally not disclosed, and the beneficiary retains managerial control of the trust and all the right to receive income and profits from the trust property.

Arms Length Regulations

Arm's Length is a transaction between parties having adverse (or opposing) interests where none of the participants are in a position to exercise substantial influence over the transaction because of business or family relationship(s) with more than one of the parties. Arms length regulations require some revocable trust (and virtually all irrevocable trusts) to utilize a disinterested third-party to act as the trustee or co-trustee to avoid the doctrine of merger (defined below). Similar to the laws of attribution, no disinterested third-party may include any member of your immediate family (father, mother, brother, sister, husband, wife, son or daughter), however arms length regulations also extend to any close friends or business contacts whose association to the trust (in a fiduciary capacity) may cause a conflict of interest and are therefore prohibited. It is prudent to consider the services of a reputable attorney, bank or company to provide fit and proper trustee services.

Doctrine of Merger

The doctrine of merger states that in the event a person is both the sole trustee and beneficiary of a trust, there is a fusing of legal and equitable title and the trust is terminated.

Equitable Title

"A title that indicates a beneficial interest in property, which gives the holder the right to acquire the formal legal title." – Black's Law Dictionary (9th Edition)

When the assets of a trust are finally disbursed, the beneficiary shall be able to exert equitable title and receive legal title to the trust property. Prior to the disbursement of the trust assets, the trustee has both legal and equitable title while the beneficiaries hold a 'beneficial interest' in the trust. Upon funding the trust, the settlor no longer has legal or equitable title as equitable title is 'vested' in the beneficiaries.

Legal Title

"A title that evidences apparent ownership but does not necessarily signify complete title or beneficial interest." – Black's Law Dictionary (9th Edition)

Legal title is given to the person (trustee) to whom title to of assets are recorded, for and on behalf of the trust (beneficiary). The legal title holder does **not** have the right to use of, nor the ability to take possession of, nor the right to collect rents or profits of, trust assets. The trustee holds legal title for an on behalf of the beneficiaries named in the trust.

Understanding Equitable and Legal Title

The distinction between legal and equitable can be difficult to understand, herein is a simple example to better understand the difference. When you receive a loan to purchase a car from a dealership, the lender (normally a bank or credit union) will hold the 'legal title' as security for payment. So, although the lender has legal title (a piece of paper), the lender cannot drive your car (make use of the asset) without your express permission.

Since you have possession of the car (physical asset), and it is registered in your name at the Department of Motor Vehicles, you have 'equitable title' and own everything except for the title document. And just as possession is 9/10 of the law, you are the owner of the car.

If you pay the lender in full, you get the legal title and would, at that time, possess both legal and equitable title to the car. If you failed to pay the lender, it would not extinguish your 'equitable interest' in the car. The lender may exercise its rights repossess the car and sell it, but they must refund any difference between the sale price at auction and the remaining balance owed on the loan. Thus, that is your 'equity'.

Powers

Trusts may be drafted to vest the power and duty of management of the trust to the beneficiary. The beneficiary then possesses the 'power of direction' to instruct the trustee what to do in relation to the trust. Such power of direction is necessary as the beneficiary does not hold legal title to the assets of the trust and must instruct the trustee when to execute documents such as deeds, mortgages and leases. Additionally, the beneficiary may possess the power to terminate and replace the trustee with another trustee (service) at any time.

Signatories

Trusts may be drafted to provide for the use of a single signatory on behalf of the settlor. This signatory (co-trustee) is the person authorized to sign documents for and on behalf of the trustee, but only upon written direction of the beneficiary. A settlor may be a co-trustee, but not be the sole signatory.

Business Preservation Trust

AssetProtectionServices.com

Business Preservation Trust

The Business Preservation Trust is a revocable business estate trust. It is designed to hold the ownership of an entity, such as the stock in a Corporation, the membership interests in a Limited Liability Company or the partnership interests in a Limited Partnership. The purpose of a Business Preservation Trust is to allow the ownership and assets of such entities to be in control of the owners while living and upon their death to pass seamlessly to the beneficiaries without ever interrupting the flow of business. The estate is transferred to the heirs by holding a shareholder / member / partner meeting to elect new officers / members / partners and bank signatories. Once there is a record of the meeting activities and the signature cards at the bank have been changed, the transfer of ownership is complete. Regardless of the size of the estate, all business assets inside the Business Preservation Trust shall transfer immediately to the beneficiaries and avoid all state and federal inheritance taxes, attorneys fees and probate. The primary benefit to creating a Business Preservation Trust is that any business assets placed into the trust are removed from an individual's personal estate, which can have tremendous estate tax benefits.

The removal of business assets out of an individual's personal estate lowers the overall value of an individual's estate. In doing so, the value of an individual's estate may fall below the estate tax exemption levels of 2011 and beyond, greatly reducing or even eliminating all personal estate taxes. For example, if the total estate of an individual were valued at $8.5 Million, federal estate taxes would consume 45% of the amount over $5 Million. The transfer of ownership of the individual's business assets valued at, say $4 Million into a business preservation trust could prevent the beneficiaries from losing as much as 45% of the $3.5 Million (or $1,575,000) in estate taxes. A business preservation trust does not replace a comprehensive revocable living trust, it compliments it. If the value of your estate is nearing a $5 Million or more, you may want to consider implementing the use of a business preservation trust for your business estate currently held in a corporation, limited liability company or limited partnership.

There are misconceptions about the ability for revocable trusts, which utilize third-party trustees, to offer asset protection capabilities. The theory is that once the assets have been funded into the trust, the settlor no longer has ownership of the assets nor the equitable and legal title and therefore need not acknowledge nor disclose ownership of the trust. Although this is true to an extent, existing court precedence state, *"If a settlor has the right to **revoke** a trust, all of the assets are treated as owned by the settlor and is ignored for creditor purposes, just as it is ignored for tax purposes."* Thus, in the event of an inside lawsuit to an entity or individual the assets in a revocable trust are within reach for a judgement creditor to seize. Failure to disclose ownership of the revocable trust could be considered 'intent to defraud a judgement creditor'. Revocable trusts are not asset protection vehicles; the primary purpose of any revocable trust is the avoidance or elimination of probate and anonymity.

Business Assets

The most advantageous way to own your business and is for the stock / membership interests / partnership interests to be 'held' by a Business Preservation trust. All your business assets such as; equipment, inventory, vehicles, accounts receivable, business property, leases and cash can automatically be transferred to the ownership of the beneficiaries of your business preservation trust when you die, avoiding state and federal inheritance taxes, lawyers and probate *no matter how large your business estate may be*.

Business Estate

Essentially a business preservation trust is a revocable inter-vivos trust much like a 'revocable living trust'. However, a business preservation trust is absolutely separate from your personal estate for the purposes of state and federal inheritance taxes and probate.

Business Estate Planning

A client shared a story where her parents had died 6 years before (when the estate tax upper limits were $2 Million per person) leaving her and her siblings a business that was then valued at $13 million dollars. After more than five years of legal entanglements, her and her siblings were 'granted' their share of the remaining estate. The total amount that was available for them all was just over $600,000 dollars. Legal fees, court costs, probate fees and taxes had eaten up $12,400,000 of the estate's value which her parents intended for her and her siblings to receive.

This is just one example of the 'theft' this generation faced. However, it didn't have to be this way. If they had a Business Preservation Trust in place at the time of their deaths, this very simple solution would have eliminated the need for her and her siblings to pay **ANY** transfer fees, **ANY** lawyer fees, **ANY** estate taxes, and there would have been **NO** probate relating to the business for them to have to endure. And best of all, the estate could have been transferred to the heirs simply by the heirs holding a shareholders / members / partners meeting, electing new officers / members / partners and bank account signatories for the Corporation / Limited Liability Company / Limited Partnership and then changing the signature card at the bank. That's it!

With a business preservation trust, your entire business estate can move on to the next generation in its totality. Your heirs are the beneficiaries of the business preservation trust and can add new beneficiaries for succeeding generations such as grandchildren and great-grandchildren. You have complete control of your business entity, its assets and its money. You can sell or add assets over time and pay for any and all normal business expenses with pre-tax dollars, including those expenditures incurred by the business preservation trust itself.

Business Preservation Trust Agreement

Under the Business Preservation Trust agreement, the trustee cannot perform any act without a letter of direction signed by a majority, if not all, of the beneficiaries or by the authorized representative (signatory for the beneficiaries). If desired by the settlor, the business preservation trust agreement can be drafted to prevent less than all of the beneficiaries from gaining control of the shares. By doing so, the trust agreement will be able to prevent a creditor who is cunning enough to attach one of the beneficiary's interests from taking control of the trust itself.

The Business Preservation Trust agreement usually designates what happens to a beneficiary interests upon death. Thus, a properly drafted Business Preservation Trust agreement will prevent any disruption in the affairs of the business estate. If one beneficiary dies, the trust agreement can specify who will be the successor to his/her beneficial interest in the trust. If there is no such designation, the beneficial interest of that person might have to be included in the deceased's estate.

Finally, beneficiaries are obligated under the trust agreement to manage, maintain and preserve the trust. A Business Preservation Trust agreement may specify which beneficiary or beneficiaries are to physically take on the responsibilities of the trust or may specify that a manager should be hired by the trust to manage the trust on behalf of the beneficiaries. All of these variations can be spelled out in the trust agreement, and the trust agreement can be amended anytime.

Beneficiary Obligations

Under the Business Preservation trust agreement, the beneficiaries agree to defend (pay for a lawyer) and indemnify (pay any claims against) the trustee for any lawsuits against the trustee arising from the trustee's management of the trust. The beneficiaries also agree to reimburse the trustee for any expenses incurred in administering the trust and/or the assets held in trust. Also there is usually a provision that any assignment of beneficial interest must be reported to (and acknowledged by) the trustee or co-trustee for the proper maintenance of the books and records of the trust.

Since the beneficiaries retain the rights and obligations of managing the trust through written directions to the trustee, these activities may create a duty to third parties. Under tort law principles, an owner or manager of the trust may be liable to third parties if his or her conduct (or lack of conduct) creates a foreseeable risk to potentially injured parties. The beneficiaries and not the trustee will be liable for the expenses related to the management and control of the trust. In addition, beneficiaries are liable for income taxes (if any) and capital gains taxes if they sell the trust assets.

Trustee Obligations

A trustee (or co-trustee) can be a person or an entity (such as a corporation, LLC or LP), who is responsible for administering and carrying out the terms of the trust and the decisions of the beneficiaries regarding the assets held in the trust. *The trustee does not hold ownership of the account, but rather acts in the capacity of a 'fiduciary' for the beneficiaries of the trust.*

The trustee has the full legal authority to sell, transfer or convey the shares as if the trustee were the owner. However, the trustee has no authority to conduct any such activities without the express prior written direction of the beneficiaries. Furthermore, the trustee generally has no right of possession or income from the shares.

Choosing a Trustee

The selection of a trustee for your Business Preservation Trust is an important decision. As the name implies, a trustee should be someone you can trust with your financial affairs. In a Business Preservation Trust, *the settlor should not be a trustee or co-trustee.*

Spartan Services as Trustee

If you 'hired' the professional disinterested third-party trustee services provided by Spartan Services then the settlor (you) could name an 'authorized signatory' (someone other than yourself) to act as a 'co-trustee'" and the signatory acting for and on behalf of the Spartan Services Such person, acting as 'co-trustee' and signatory, would sign corporate / company / partnership documents but *only* the name of Spartan Services would appear on contracts and be in the public record (if any). This acting signatory would take on the role of the 'managing trustee but **must** receive prior written approval from Spartan Services. (the Trustee of Record) before undertaking *any* matter that would be considered beyond the scope of normal day-to-day business operations of the trust.

You or Your Spouse as Trustee

Although it is technically possible for you or your spouse to act as the Trustee or Co-Trustee of a Business Preservation Trust, it is strongly advised that you do not do so for the following reasons. First, under Nevada Trust Law, it is **not** possible for a settlor to be a trustee (or co-trustee) *and* a beneficiary. Such a structure would violate the 'doctrine of merger' and would be considered a 'sham'. Second, even if you or your spouse were not beneficiaries, acting as a trustee or co-trustee would defeat a very important aspect to the business preservation trust, which is anonymity.

Concealing ownership from the prying eyes of legal predators is of tremendous benefit and should not be overlooked. If someone is thinking of suing you or your Corp / LLC / LP, and the business assets were titled "Your Name, as trustee (or authorized signatory for the trustee) of the XYZ Trust," it doesn't take a genius to find you or figure out the connection. Although asset protection benefits are provided by the entity under state law, the business preservation trust provides a 'vail of anonymity' which can proactively help to avoid lawsuits.

And lastly, it is not advisable for you or your spouse to act as the trustee or co-trustee of a business preservation trust as there are situations in which you cannot 'hide' from judgement creditors. For example, if you are deposed by a creditor or placed under oath in a debtor's exam (where you are prohibited by law from pleading your 5th Amendment rights) you would be required to disclose information about the trust including divulging the beneficiaries. If the trustee is difficult to locate (and/or resides in another state), it makes it far more difficult and expensive for any judgment creditors to obtain information about the trust, or more importantly the trust's assets.

Attorney or CPA as Trustee

Attorneys and Certified Public Accountants (CPA's) are good choices for trustee as they generally provide client privilege and may further protect the element of privacy. The down side of using attorneys or CPA's as trustee are their fees can get excessive and, coupled with a potential negative attitude toward the operation of a Business Preservation Trust (due to lack of knowledge) should be taken into consideration before choosing them as your trustee.

Business Associates, Friends or Relatives as Trustee

Business associates, friends or relatives (other than a spouse) are another viable option for trustee because of the integrity factor. In most states you can use a trustee (or co-trustee) that resides in a state different than the one in which trust has established as its situs. *Remember, a trustee that is hard to find helps keep your ownership private.*

Should you opt for a business associate, friend or relative as trustee, make certain they are someone who is knowledgeable in financial matters. Choose someone who is reliable, stable and readily available (to you) for executing documents.

In-laws *may* be another choice because they are family, but should have a different last name from yours. However, if you have marital problems, in-law may decide to take matters into their own hands and could act in a manner not befitting the fiduciary capacity of the trustee and place the family's best interest above yours (or the trust).

Entity as Trustee

In some states, if an entity (such as a corporation) is acting as trustee it must be registered with the Secretary of State as a trust company to serve as a trustee. In those states, this could preclude you from using your own corporation to act as trustee.

Replacing a Trustee

A Business Preservation Trust is a revocable instrument, and so the agreement may be revised and/or the trustee may be terminated at anytime while you are alive. A trust created during your lifetime (the lifetime of the settlor) provides an opportunity to test the reliability of your trustee. You obviously cannot discharge the trustee once you are deceased, but you certainly can while you are still alive.

Tips for Choosing a Trustee

The further away the trustee resides, the more difficult it will be for outsiders to deal with the trust and/or the trustee. The only way a trustee should reveal the identity of the beneficiaries is pursuant to a court order or if otherwise required by law. *Keep in mind that a court order is only valid in the state in which it is issued.* If your trustee resides in a different state, it will be much more difficult for an attorney trying to serve process on the trustee.

Trustee Obligations to the Beneficiaries

Trustee duties and obligations arise from the trust agreement and general trust law principles. The Business Preservation Trust agreement lists specific duties and obligations for the trustee. The following is a brief summary of those obligations:

- To hold title to the Shares for the benefit of the beneficiaries;
- To protect and conserve the Shares:
- Not to reveal the identity of the beneficiaries;
- Not to record the trust agreement in the public records unless required to do so:
- Not to execute any legal documents without the direction of the beneficiaries:
- To maintain records of the names and addresses of the beneficiaries and the amount of their beneficial interest in the Business Preservation Trust;
- To resign and hand over books and records if his/her activities are terminated by the beneficiaries, by the terms of the trust agreement or by law; and
- To execute any sales contracts, leases, options, etc. at the direction of the beneficiaries.

Trustee Liabilities to Third-Parties

Generally, a trustee is not liable to third parties for acts perpetrated within the scope of duties as trustee, so long as the trustee discloses representative capacity. Furthermore, most states have laws that protect a trustee from personal liability for activities carried out in furtherance of the trust.

A properly drafted trust agreement states that any debts or obligations incurred by the trustee for the trust shall be obligations of the trust. Since the trustee and the beneficiaries are not partners or agents of each other, they do not have the power or authority to bind one another for obligations. Any obligation, which the trustee incurs for the trust remains the obligation of the trust itself and thereby the beneficiaries. Despite any of the foregoing, a trustee (or co-trustee) should always make it unmistakable to third parties to be acting in a representative capacity. The trustee should create a stamp with this language pre-printed on it so as to properly sign all documents.

> ### Name of Trustee
> *Authorized Signatory for the*
> *Spartan Services (Trustee of Record)*
> *All parties dealing with said the Trust or Trustee*
> *Must look solely to the assets of the trust*

Power of Direction

The Business Preservation Trust vests the power and duty of management of the trust assets in the beneficiaries while a typical trust vests all power in the trustee. The beneficiaries have the 'power of direction' to tell the trustee what to do in relation to the trust property. This power of direction is necessary because the beneficiaries do not have legal title and thus must direct the trustee to execute documents such as deeds, mortgages and leases. The beneficiaries maintain the power to terminate the trustee at will, if they deem it necessary.

The Business Preservation Trust provides for the use of an 'authorized signatory' of the settlor's choosing (may not be the settlor) to sign documents for and on behalf of the trustee. Such an authorized signatory is the co-trustee. This authorized signatory is the *only* person who will be authorized to sign documents and may *only* execute documents upon receiving written direction from the beneficiaries. This requirement further establishing the beneficiaries' control and power of direction over the trusts assets.

Tax Returns

A Business Preservation Trust is not required to have an Employer Identification Number (EIN), a bank account or file tax returns **unless** the entity declares a dividend or receives income, at which point the then living settlor or beneficiaries must file a tax return and pay the appropriate taxes, if any.

There is no known Internal Revenue Code that '*requires*' an entity to declare and pay a dividend or make a distribution on its net income. The entity may pay taxes on its retained earnings, which is preferable to distributing profits for a business preservation trust. Bear in mind that the trust beneficiaries '*own*' the assets of the entity, which naturally would include the entity's bank account and so there is really no need to distribute funs to the trust anyway. The settlor of the business preservation trust should *not* be a beneficiary because when the settlor / beneficiary dies his or her portion of the trust (estate) would most likely have to be probated and/or taxed.

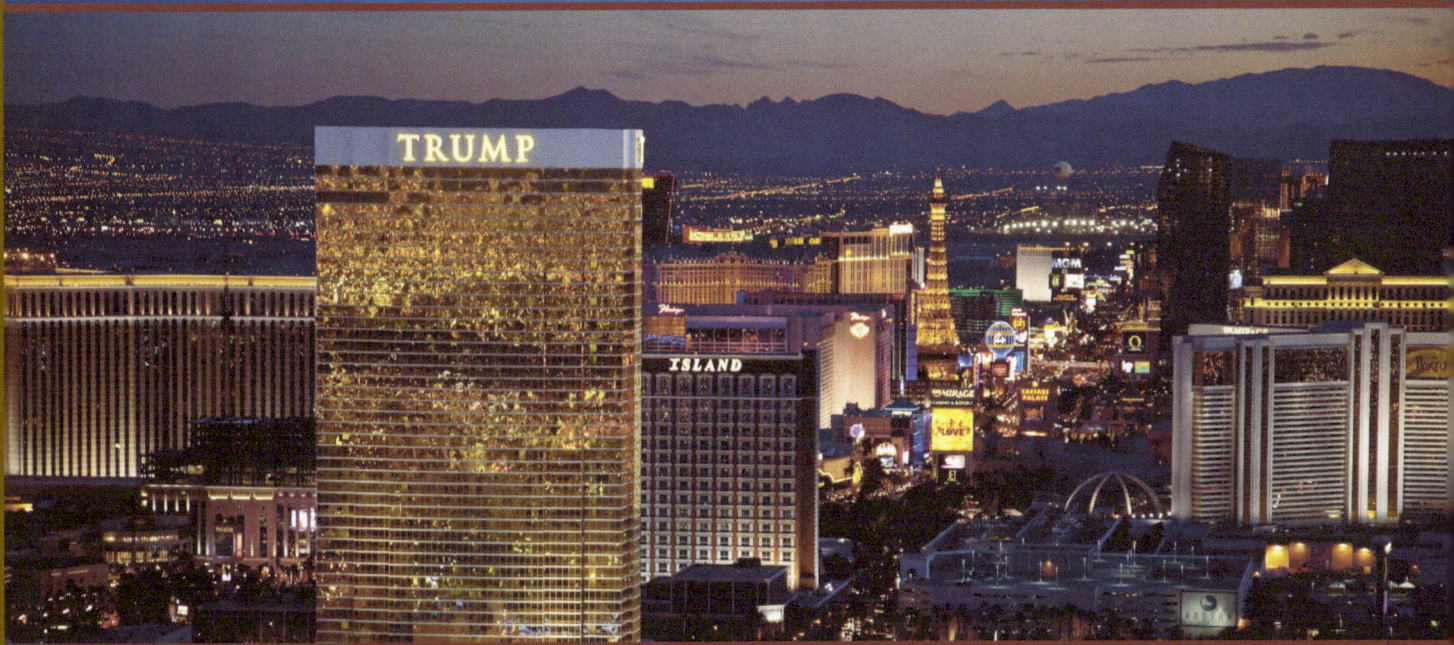

Personal Property Trusts

AssetProtectionServices.com

Personal Property Trusts

A Personal Property Trust (PPT) is similar to a land trust or living trust in that a Personal Property Trust is a form of a revocable trust. The primary object of a Personal Property Trust is not asset protection, but to furnish as much privacy as possible to discourage or even avoid meritless litigation. A PPT is a very effective tool which can be utilized in a variety of methods and affords key advantages.

The beneficial owners of a Personal Property Trust are not a matter of public record. Meaning, a PPT provides what could be termed a "double-blind" veil of invisibility in that the trust agreement is neither formed nor recorded with any state agency. So with only a generic trust name from which to begin an investigation, potential creditors are quickly discouraged at the thought of having to unearth the proper ownership identity and location from a countless number of such trusts. Whatever assets have been placed into a PPT affords the owners tremendous privacy.

Bank Accounts and Securities

Non-publicly recorded assets, such as bank accounts and securities, can be placed into a Personal Property Trust. If a judgement is ever entered against you, the creditor would likely be unable to attachment the judgement to any personal property not titled in your name.

Entity Ownership

Personal Property Trusts are very effective in holding the shares to a corporation, membership interests in a limited liability company, or partnership interests in a limited partnership. The use of a Personal Property Trust can also be an excellent means of adding additional layers of anonymity to the identity of an LLC managing member listed in the public domain on a Secretary of State website.

Land Trusts

Land trusts are one of the best tools to hold title to your real estate. However, some title companies and/or lenders may request the disclosure of the beneficiaries of the trust before insuring title, insurance policies or funding a loan from a lender. In these cases, you can use the Personal Property Trust as the beneficiary of the land trust. By doing so you are in essence "embedding" one trust into another. As a result, even if you do reveal the beneficiary, it's just another trust and neither you nor or an entity would be disclosed.

Some states require the beneficial interest holder of a land trust be disclosed. A Personal Property Trust is the perfect tool to act as the beneficial interest holder of your land trust creating an additional layer of anonymity between your land trust and the entity holding the ultimate beneficial interest of your property. And even if an interested attorney were able to obtain the name of the entity holding the ultimate beneficial interest, they would not be able to find you as an officer or directors of the company, at least in states such as Nevada and Wyoming which still permit nominees.

Mortgages and Options

When you purchase real property you can lend money to yourself (or an entity you own) which is secured by the real estate being purchased. Lending money secured by real property is called a mortgage, and mortgages are considered assets to the "lender". Just as with a mortgage, when you place an option on the purchase of real property, such information is generally recorded in the public records. The information contained is available for any interested person to see and investigate. So, rather than placing a mortgage or an option directly into your name (or the name of your company), consider holding a mortgage or option in the name of a Personal Property Trust to ensure a higher level of privacy.

One consideration is to create and record mortgages against any real estate you may own using a different Personal Property Trust (i.e. mortgage) for each property. To anyone running an asset search on you (or your company), your real property would appear encumbered and make anyone considering suing you think twice about pursuing someone who appears broke and indebted!

Motor Vehicles

Whenever you purchase a car, boat, truck, mobile-home, motor-home or other type of motor vehicle, the ownership information is generally recorded publicly with the Department of Motor Vehicles (DMV). Almost every DMV allows an individual to record up to three (3) assets into a Personal Property Trust, thus providing you helpful anonymity. In most states, only the name of the Trust need appear on the Title, Registration and Proof of Insurance with the name and contact information of the Trustee being an optional disclosure.

Revocable Living Trusts

AssetProtectionServices.com

Revocable Living Trust

Revocable Living Trusts provided by Asset Protection Services of America are current with estate planning and estate tax laws throughout the United States and the District of Columbia at the time of creation and can be updated annually. A living trust is a powerful estate planning device which should be created for the purpose of avoiding probate, guardianship, conservatorship and to reduce or eliminate federal and state estate taxes. Living trusts are *not* a vehicle for reducing income tax or protecting assets.

The distribution of your estate assets are directed by the Revocable Living Trust according to your last wishes and desires without the need for your beneficiaries to succumb the lengthy emotional court proceedings and expensive attorney's fees. Living trusts are effective during your lifetime whereas 'wills' and 'testamentary trusts' take effect upon your death and instantly send beneficiaries into probate. Whatever is properly placed into your Revocable Living Trust prior to your death prevents family, friends and beneficiaries from going through probate.

- ✓ You act as trustee of your revocable living trust and maintain full control over your assets during your lifetime.
- ✓ You can amend your revocable living trust at any time to allow for changes in your family, economic circumstances or for changes in the law.
- ✓ A revocable living trust is generally neither recorded nor registered with any public agency, so it is private and not public.
- ✓ A revocable living trust allows immediate implementation of your estate plan.
- ✓ A revocable living trust provides immediate distribution of your assets or directs the assets to be held in trust for an extended period of time.
- ✓ A revocable living trust does not pay any additional income taxes and no separate federal or state income tax returns need be filed while you act as trustee.

When you create a living trust you can act as your own trustee so there are no management fees or loss of control. You can change or modify the trust terms at any time, change beneficiaries and add or delete assets held by the trust without tax consequences. So long as you are the trustee of your Living Trust, you file your income tax returns exactly as before the trust existed. There are no new returns to file and no new tax liabilities are created.

A Revocable Living Trust does not complicate the management of your assets. You can do whatever you can do now with your assets and property including buying, selling, borrowing and making gifts, etc. A living trust Records Book should be kept in a prominent location, such as a home office bookshelf, with an easy-to-read spine labelled "Living Trust" so that it may be quickly located by immediate family members in the event of an untimely death. The introductory portion of a living trust should include updated contact information of friends, employers, professional advisors, document locations, and declaration of final arrangements.

Types of Revocable Living Trusts

There are a number of different trust types for a married couple; all of which are typified by the result after the first death. The factors which go into determining the correct type of trust are the size of the estate, tax laws, underlying ownership of the trust assets and comfort levels expressed by the couple with regards to the degree of control the survivor should have over the trust. You are not required to try to figure out the correct type of trust for you; our software will determine which is the best trust for your situation using our unique "matrix" which analyses your responses to certain certain questions, as well as the most up-to-date status of the federal and state tax laws.

Revocable Trusts

Use a Revocable Living Trust for personal effects (artwork, books, cameras, computers, clothing, collectibles, furniture, jewelry, sporting equipment, etc), your personal residence, personal vehicles and personal bank accounts. Land Trusts hold real property, other than your principle residency, and Business Preservation Trusts hold your stock in a Corporation, membership interests in an LLC and limited partnership interests in an LP.

Irrevocable Trusts

Irrevocable trusts are **not** convenient as they are permanent and cannot be modified, changed or revoked. However, it is for these very reasons, irrevocable trusts provide excellent asset protection. Irrevocable trusts are entities and considered 'persons' with separate legal personalities. Living Trusts are revocable until the time of your death, at which point they become irrevocable and, although the irrevocability of the trust does not serve an asset protection purpose at that time (because you're dead), a revocable living trust cannot be modified, changed or revoked upon your death.

'A/B' Trust

An "A/B Trust" is called that because, at the first death, the joint trust splits into two sub-trusts (originally labeled the "A Trust" and the "B Trust". The deceased spouse's sub-trust (which we call the "Decedent's Trust") is funded up to the maximum amount which can pass tax free in the year of death (currently $5M) and the surviving spouse's sub-trust (named as the "Survivor's Trust") receives the balance. The Decedent's Trust is irrevocable and is held for the lifetime of the surviving spouse. Typically, the survivor is the sole trustee and has the right to all of the income and the right to invade any or all of the principal of the sub-trust for her/his benefit. However, this sub-trust can be protected from creditors of the surviving spouse (including the "spend-down" for Medicaid) and the survivor cannot leave the assets of the Decedent's Trust to anyone other than the children. The balance in the Survivor's Trust qualifies for the unlimited marital deduction and no tax is due at the first death. At the death of the survivor what is in the Survivor's Trust is subject to tax, but only to the extent that the total is above the exemption amount in the year of the survivor's death. The Decedent's Trust, because it was already subject to tax at the first death and because it is an irrevocable trust, passes estate tax free at the second death. Because of the higher exemption amount and the loss of a potential income tax benefit at the death of the surviving spouse, this type of trust is not recommended for most situations (it may still be beneficial for "non-traditional" couples).

'ABC' Trust

The "ABC Trust" is another version of the 'Marital Deduction Trust' and has the excess of the deceased spouse's estate above the exemption amount going to another sub-trust often called a QTIP (Qualified Terminable Interest Property Trust) which we label as the "Marital Deduction Trust". The decedent's trust is an irrevocable trust held for the lifetime of the surviving spouse. Typically, the survivor is the sole trustee and has the right to all of the income and the right to use any or all of the principal of the trust for her/his benefit; however, the survivor cannot leave the trust to anyone other than the beneficiaries initially named. The balance of the assets not allocated into the two irrevocable trusts are placed in the Survivor's Trust which qualifies for the unlimited marital deduction and results in no estate tax at the first death. At the death of the survivor, what is in the Survivor's Trust is subject to tax, but only to the extent that the total is above the exemption amount in the year of the survivor's death. The Decedent's Trust, because it was already subject to tax at the first death and because it is an irrevocable trust, passes estate tax free at the second death. The Marital Deduction Trust is only subject to tax to the extent that it and the Survivor's Trust exceeds the available exemption amount at the time of the survivor's death.

'Disclaimer' Trust

A "Disclaimer Trust" which is similar to the probate avoidance trust except the surviving spouse has the opportunity to disclaim any portion of the decedent's estate into an irrevocable tax avoidance sub-trust. This sub-trust is created (if necessary) by the terms of the trust after the first death and then passes tax free at the survivor's death. This is a very useful trust given the uncertainty of the estate tax laws and the likelihood that most estates will not actually require the creation of a separate trust for tax purposes. A 'disclaimer trust' defers the decision of what estate tax planning is necessary until the time of the first death when the size of the estate and the exact nature of the tax laws are clearly defined. Typically, this type of trust is utilized when there is no concern with the survivor having full control over the trust.

'Marital Deduction' Trust

With the new 2010 Tax Relief Act, a new type of trust called a "Marital Deduction Trust" is now our recommended choice for many estates. At the first death, the joint trust again splits into two sub-trusts; the deceased spouse's sub-trust (which we call the "Decedent's Trust") is funded with the deceased spouse's estate up to the maximum amount which can pass tax free in the year of death (currently $5M) and the "Survivor's Trust" receives the survivor's estate. As with the "A/B Trust", the Decedent's Trust is irrevocable and is held for the lifetime of the surviving spouse (typically, the survivor is the sole trustee and has the right to all of the income and the right to use any or all of the principal of the sub-trust for her/his benefit); as with the A/B Trust, this sub-trust can be protected from creditors of the surviving spouse (including the "spend-down" for Medicaid) and survivor cannot leave the assets of the Decedent's Trust to anyone other than the children. The balance in the Survivor's Trust qualifies for the unlimited marital deduction and no tax is due at the first death. At the death of the survivor, because the Decedent's Trust is treated as part of the survivor's taxable estate (even though no tax must be paid), the assets in this trust receive a new basis adjustment (a "step-up") and the heirs can sell the entire estate with no capital gains tax.

'Non-Traditional Couple' Trust

You have the option to prepare a "Joint Trust" along with all of the matching supporting documents for a "Non-traditional Couple". We will determine the best type of Trust for you after taking into account your estate tax situation. Please note that only a legally married man and woman can use the Federal Estate Tax "unlimited marital deduction"; this means that, although the full exemption [currently $5M] is available at the first death, if the deceased party's estate is greater than the exemption, there will be a tax due at the first death (even with the trust). However, by properly structuring the trust, you can keep the exemption amount from being taxed at the second death (which means the two of you can leave up to $10M in assets free of Federal Estate Tax.

'Probate Avoidance' Trust

A "Probate Avoidance Trust" continues everything in a single trust for the benefit of the survivor who maintains complete right of change and/or revocability. Typically, this type of a trust is utilized when there will be no possibility of estate tax and there is no issue about control the survivor will have over the entire trust.

'Qualified Domestic' Trust

A non-citizen surviving spouse can cause issues and may be required to pay substantial estate taxes at the first death if a proper estate plan is not in place. Depending on the size of the estate, it may be necessary to have your Living Trust set up as a "Qualified Domestic Trust" to avoid the payment of any taxes at the first death. We will create the appropriate trust for you based on the information you provide in the assembly process.

Avoiding Probate

An object of primary concern is the avoidance of probate. If your estate is over your state's "small estate" limit, then your estate must go through the expense and delay of a court administered probate proceeding at your death. Probate is a court procedure whereby upon your death your assets are distributed according to your will, or by state law if you have no will. A Will is a legal document that describes how your assets should be distributed in the event of death. The actual distribution is controlled by a legal process called probate, which is Latin for "prove the will." Upon your death, the Will must be filed with the Probate Court and becomes a public document available for inspection. If you have no Will, the government's estate plan is called "Intestacy" and guarantees government interference in the disposition of your estate. Documents must be filed to appoint an 'approved' administrator and then filed with the Probate Court.

Additionally, consider estate taxes. There is much you can do in planning your estate that will reduce and can even eliminate estate taxes. A Living Trust will not save any death taxes for an individual unless other deductions are available (for example, if you give a portion of your assets to charity). Saving on estate taxes is just one of the benefits of a Living Trust. Further, estate taxes have no bearing on the protections which a Living Trust (along with the appropriate health care power and general power of attorney) can provide in the event of your incapacity.

When an estate goes through probate, probate assets are frozen until the Court approves the executor and the Will. Creditors are invited to come forward with their claims and heirs may challenge certain bequests under the Will if they are disappointed because they received less than they had anticipated. With a living trust, assets are not frozen and can be distributed to your designated beneficiaries immediately and a disgruntled heir would have to hire an attorney and file a civil suit against each beneficiary.

Probate court is *not* a private proceeding but rather a public event where assets are often frozen and prohibited from being distributed without a court order. The *average* estate takes 1.5 years before the probate process is finally over. If your estate contains real estate in multiple jurisdictions, ancillary probates are held in each respective state wherein the properties are located. There are many disadvantages to probate including the costs to your family and friends for attorneys, appraisers, real estate agents and independent administrators. And should any problems arise, extensive time delays must be taken into consideration as courts may extend probate for years to resolve conflicts and disputes. If probate can be avoided or eliminated, all reasonable measures should be taken to do so.

Certificate of Revocable Living Trust

A certificate of revocable living trust provides the trustee of your living trust the means to present third-parties such a document articulating the powers granted to the trustee without the need for disclosing the entire trust agreement to the public.

Continuity of Management

Creating a living trust can furnish needed attention to your assets. A living trust permits you and/or your appointed trustee to take timely advantage of investment opportunities and conversely, to dispose of investments no longer desirable. With a living trust, you set up the machinery to provide a continuity of management at death and the immediate shift of income from yourself to your beneficiaries at your death.

Continuity of Personal Affairs

Unfortunately, if you become mentally disabled before you die, you may become the subject of a conservatorship or guardianship proceeding where the probate court can appoint someone to take control of your assets and personal affairs. These court-appointed agents must file a strict accounting of your finances with the court. A Living Trust will help avoid this process because your assets are titled in the trust; and you have already appointed someone to act as the successor trustee of your trust if you are no longer able to act. Additionally, if you have created a Durable Power of Attorney and Health Care power; you have already given someone else the ability to make both financial and health care decisions on your behalf. In short, with a properly drafted and complete estate plan, you can eliminate the need for a guardianship or conservatorship.

Eliminate Problems of Guardianship or Control

With a trust, when minors are the beneficiaries, the trustee can manage and invest the trust funds free of the costs and restrictions that arise when a court must appoint and supervise a guardian of the property until the beneficiary comes of age (at age 18). Additionally, with a trust, you can continue the management of a beneficiary's assets to whatever age you desire; certainly beyond age 18.

The management of a beneficiary's assets can include disbursement of assets and/or funds in increments, according to the directions you put in the trust (e.g., 1/3 distribution at age 25, 1/3 distribution at age 30, and the balance at age 35). Of course, the trustee can use any or all of the trust principal for the benefit of the beneficiary during this period for health, support, care and education. Also, if there is any question of management skills or capacity of the beneficiary, or to insure that your estate does not go to a son-in-law or a daughter-in-law, the trust can continue for the child's lifetime and then pass to the child's issue at his or her death. This will also keep your assets in your family rather than having them be subject to attachment by creditors or by the state for medical treatment. You can protect the assets from any potential of dissipation of the entire estate while providing for the beneficiary's needs, as determined by you. With a living trust, these trusts are already in place at the time of your death and will begin immediately for the benefit and protection of your beneficiaries.

Directives to Physicians

Physician's directives provide instruction for your family medical doctor should you have an incurable condition caused by injury, disease or illness where life-sustaining procedures would serve to artificially prolong the moment of death. A properly drafted living trust should provide a 'directive to physicians' for the right to continue to fight for life, to end artificial life-prolongment immediately or after a set period of time, or for your attorney-in-fact to decide on your behalf when or if to pull-the-plug after weighing the facts presented by your physician and attending medical doctors.

Digital Assets

Your digital assets and/or rights (including any "social media", on-line accounts and/or email accounts) will be automatically transferred to the Trust with the "Assignment of Personal Property" (created as part of the trust package); both the trust and the Durable General Power of Attorney also specifically authorize the Trustee and Agent to deal with digital assets and/or rights. However, it is important to maintain a list of all of your digital assets and print it out on paper; this list should include all of your on-line accounts as well as a list of usernames and passwords. This is sensitive information, so protect this information by keeping it in a secure place. Some people will put this information in a sealed envelope to be opened only upon death or incapacity. Wherever you keep this information, make sure you tell your successor Trustee (and agent under the Power of Attorney, if different) where this information can be found. You should update this list at least yearly. In addition, tell your successor Trustee what you want done with your digital assets. If you have a social networking site, such as Facebook, LinkedIn or Twitter let your successor Trustee know whether you want the site maintained following your death or whether you want the site removed (some sites have specific policies regarding what happens when a person dies or is incapacitated, so make sure you check each site's policy). If you have a collection of music or photographs, tell your successor Trustee what you want done with those.

HIPAA

New federal regulations known as the Health Insurance Portability and Accountability Act ("HIPAA") imposes strict privacy regulations on the disclosure of individually identifiable health information. This necessitates the addition of specific release and consent authority in all health care powers before any health care provider can release medical information to your agents and interested persons. Because HIPAA has no "grandfather" exceptions, previously executed estate planning documents may now be useless unless the documents specifically address the HIPAA requirements. All heath care documents and the living trust included in our program are specifically HIPAA compliant and the HIPAA release provisions are made effective immediately.

Last Will and Testament
("Pour-Over Will")

The last will and testament is a catch-all for any assets which may have been neglected to be placed into the living trust during the course of a person's lifetime. Upon death, this instruments directs those assets to pour-over into the comprehensive revocable living trust thus avoiding probate for the remainder of the residual estate.

Living Will

A Living Will provides specific 'Directives for Physicians' in the event you are incapacitated or disabled to the point where you body is in a coma or on some form of life support (e.g., Alzheimer's, a stroke, an accident, etc.) and you are unable to communicate your wishes to others. So, in laymen's terms, the document allows your "will" or desires to be respected while you are still living even though you may be unconscious or unable to communicate.

Pet Trust

You can create a "Pet Trust" as an option; this trust can be for a specific animal or animals or for whatever animals survive you. You can designate different trustees for the care of the pet and the amount allocated for the care of the animal. You will also have the option to designate a trust "enforcer"; this person is a third party who has the right to make sure the funds are actually being used for the care of the animal.

Power of Attorney

A creditor can file for a receivership or conservatorship in the court that they be allowed to handle your personal and financial affairs. Disadvantages include the need to hire an attorney and the subsequent costs for legal representation. Expect delays spanning from a few weeks to months or even years. This process is public and not private, and the court is in control of your estate and monitors everything you do. The court may also require restrictions on whomever handles your affairs. Various powers of attorney eliminate these problems. You decide whom to appoint and nobody may second-guess your decision. You or your loved ones will not have to go to court. There are no time delays for the person of your choice to take over your affairs when you are unable to. There are no court reports and only the person you choose will have control over your assets until you are able to handle them yourself.

Special Power of Attorney

The Special Power of Attorney for Assets enables the attorney-in-fact (agent) of your choosing to present such a document to third-parties to articulate and clarify the specific powers granted to the agent to transfer and convey assets standing in your name into your revocable living trust.

General Power of Attorney

The General Power of Attorney for Property gives sweeping powers to the agent of your choosing to act on your behalf on a broad spectrum of areas. Virtually every aspect of your life could be handled by the person to whom you chose to entrust such powers should you become mentally incapable of continuing to manage your financial affairs.

Durable Power of Attorney

The Durable Power of Attorney for Health Care gives a comprehensive range of powers to the agent of your choosing to act on your behalf with doctors, hospitals and other agencies in the event that your personal physician declares you, in writing, to be physically incapable of managing your own health care affairs.

Restated Amendments

If there are any changes in federal and/or state law which may affect your trust, you will receive notification. Should a change be necessary, you can create a Restated Amendment at any time in the future. If there have been any legal changes which could affect your trust a 'Restated Amendment' completely rewrites your estate plan to have all the new language to keep your trust current. Restated Amendments keep your existing trust name and date, so you do not need to re-title any of the assets already titled in the name of the existing trust.

State Estate Taxes

States may levy an estate tax, which is allowed under the federal estate tax laws, in the exact amount of the Internal Revenue Code Section 2011. Beneficiaries are subject to different inheritance tax rates and exemptions based on their relationship to the decedent. Such estate taxes imposed by the states are often called a "pick-up" tax. Many states have annual budget deficits in the hundreds of millions of dollars, some in the billions and aggressively look to generate or pick-up revenue to help cover such losses.

American Taxpayer Relief Act (ATRA)

On January 2nd, 2013 President Barack Hussein Obama signed the American Taxpayer Relief Act (ATRA) which created permanent changes to federal rules governing estate taxes, gift taxes and generation skipping transfer taxes previously implemented under the 2010 "Tax Relief Unemployment Insurance Reauthorization and Job Creation Act" (TRUIRJCA). The 2014 'coupon' for individual taxpayers under ATRA is $5,340,000 and scheduled to increase annually based on inflation. Meaning, if the value of an individual's net estate (which is the gross estate reduced by allowable estate tax credits and deductions) does not exceed $5.34 Million, then the estate will pass to the heirs free from federal estate taxes.

Tax Reduction or Elimination

For married grantors, the estate tax liability, which would otherwise be due at the death of the survivor, can be greatly reduced or completely eliminated by proper planning. This planning can be accomplished in a living trust (although it can also be accomplished through wills, this would require a separate probate at the death of each spouse). How much can be saved depends on the size of the estate and the estate tax laws at the time of the surviving spouse's death. A revocable living trust can also insure that the estate of the first spouse to die will ultimately go to his or her children or heirs; even though the surviving spouse is provided the lifetime economic benefit of all assets and has complete management and control over the entire trust.

Trust Agreement

The trust agreement is the core of your living trust and details to whom your remainder estate shall be given, and under what time frames or conditions. In addition to clearly articulating fiduciary powers and responsibilities, a well written trust agreement should provide means of accessing information efficiently and effectively.

Trust Conditions

There can be no conditions in the trust agreement that would prevent a qualifying beneficiary from eventually receiving his or her share of the estate after you and your spouse die. For example, it is not permissible to state. "My daughter shall receive her inheritance only when she removes that ring from her nose," or "My son shall receive his inheritance when he graduates from medical school," because should these events never occur, the beneficiary would not receive his or her share of the estate.

Who Should Be a Beneficiary?

Spouse as Beneficiary

Most married people, especially those who have been married for some time, name their spouse as beneficiary. And, in most cases, this will be your best option. The two main reasons are:

1. the money will be available to provide for your surviving spouse, and
2. it gives you the spousal rollover option.

If your spouse is more than ten years younger than you are, you can use a different life expectancy chart that will make your required distributions less, allowing tax-deferred growth to continue longer on more money.

Spousal Rollover Options

If you die first, your surviving spouse can 'roll-over' your tax-deferred account into his or her own IRA further delaying income taxes until such time as your spouse must start taking the required minimum distributions. When your spouse utilizes the rollover, he or she names a new beneficiary, preferably a much younger one, such as your children and/or grandchildren. After your spouse dies, the beneficiary's actual life expectancy will be used for the remaining required minimum distributions. Depending on the beneficiary's age at that time that could mean decades of tax-deferred growth. Under the new rules, if your spouse dies first you can name a new beneficiary and, after you die, the distributions will be based on the new beneficiary's life expectancy.

A potential disadvantage of naming your spouse as beneficiary is that your spouse will have full control of the money, which may not be what you want. You may have children from a previous marriage or feel that others may too easily influence your spouse after you're gone. The spouse doesn't have to utilize a rollover and, if easily coerced, the spouse could take a lump-sum distribution, even if all the income taxes would have to be paid at once at that time.

Naming your spouse as beneficiary may also cause you to pay too much in estate taxes. If your estate is large enough to pay estate taxes and most of your estate is made up of your tax-deferred savings, naming your spouse as the beneficiary could cause you to waste all or part of your exemption. If you have other assets that can be applied to your exemption, this may not be a problem. If your spouse becomes incapacitated, the court could take control of this money or it could also be lost to your spouse's creditors.

Children as Beneficiary

If your spouse will have plenty of assets or if you have reason to believe your spouse will die before you, you could name your children, grandchildren or other individuals as beneficiary.

The tax benefits can be great. Since you are not leaving this money to your spouse, your estate tax exemption can be applied to it saving on estate taxes. And if your beneficiary is much younger than you (as your children and grandchildren would be), you can get the maximum 'stretch-out' on tax-deferred growth. However, any time you name an individual as a beneficiary, you lose control. After you die, your beneficiary can do whatever he or she wants with this money, including cashing out the entire account and destroying your carefully made plans for long-term, tax-deferred growth.

There is the risk of court interference at incapacity too. Money that has been withdrawn would be available to the beneficiary's creditors, spouse and ex-spouse(s). And if you leave a substantial amount to a grandchild, it could be subject to the generation skipping transfer tax, which is equal to the highest estate tax rate in effect at that time and is in addition to estate and income taxes. For maximum control (especially with a minor or irresponsible individual), consider naming your revocable living trust as the beneficiary instead.

Advantages to a Revocable Living Trust as Beneficiary

Naming your Revocable Living Trust as the beneficiary will give you the maximum control over your tax-deferred money after you die. That's because the distributions will be paid not to an individual, but into your Living Trust, which contains your written instructions stating who will receive this money, and when.

With an A-B Living Trust as beneficiary, you can provide for your surviving spouse for as long as he or she lives, yet keep control over who receives the money after your spouse dies. Plus the proceeds can be used to satisfy your estate tax exemption and save on estate taxes. Your Living Trust could also provide periodic income to your children or grandchildren, keeping the rest safe from irresponsible spending and/or creditors.

While you are living, the required minimum distributions will be paid to you over your life expectancy (determined from the Uniform Lifetime Table). After you die, the required distributions can be paid to the Living Trust over the life expectancy of the oldest beneficiary of the Living Trust. Just as you can do now, the Trustee of your Living Trust will be able to withdraw more money from the account if needed to follow the instructions in your Living Trust, but the rest can stay in the account and continue to grow tax-deferred. You can, of course, name anyone you wish as Trustee. But if the Living Trust will exist for a long period of time (for example, to provide for your grandchildren), you may want to consider a corporate Trustee.

Disadvantages to a Revocable Living Trust as Beneficiary

Disadvantages to consider with a Revocable Living Trust as beneficiary include not being able to provide for your spouse and stretch out the tax-deferred growth beyond your spouse's actual life expectancy. Remember, after you die the distributions will be paid over the life expectancy of the oldest beneficiary of the Living Trust. If your spouse is a beneficiary of your Living Trust, he or she will probably be the oldest beneficiary. If your spouse is not a beneficiary of the Living Trust, the oldest beneficiary may be one of your children. That would let you extend the tax deferral over your child's life expectancy, but the money wouldn't be available to your spouse.

After you pass, income that stays in a Revocable Living Trusts is subject to paying income taxes at a higher rate than most individuals. Distributions from your tax-deferred account that are paid to the Living Trust are subject to income tax and if they were to stay in the Living Trust the higher tax rates would apply. Although generally this is not the case because the Trustee distributes the income to the beneficiaries of the Living Trust, who then pay the income tax at their own (usually lower) rates.

Revocable Living Trust as Beneficiary of a Tax-Deferred Account

In order for a Revocable Living Trust to be beneficiary of a tax-deferred account, it should at least meet the following requirements:

1. It must be valid under state law;
2. It must be irrevocable (revocable living trusts become irrevocable at your death)
3. The beneficiaries must be individuals and identifiable from the Living Trust document.
4. A copy of the Living Trust document and any subsequent revisions must be provided to the Plan Administrator or IRA Trustee, custodian or issuer.

Depending on the kind of Living Trust you would like to use, there may be additional regulations governing them. Check with your state attorney.

Charity or Foundation as Beneficiary

If you are planning to leave assets to a charity after you die, a tax-deferred account can be an excellent tool to use. That's because when you name a charity as the beneficiary; there will be no income or estate taxes on this money after you die.

If you name a Charitable Remainder Trust (CRT) as a beneficiary, your spouse, children or others can receive an income for a set number of years or for as long as they live, and you will still save income and estate taxes. You can also set up your own charitable foundation and have the foundation pay your kids a salary to run it. Under new rules, even with a charity as your beneficiary, you use the Uniform Lifetime Table to determine your required minimum distributions. But you still need to be aware of a charity's 'zero' life expectancy.

Combination of Beneficiaries

You don't have to choose just one of the aforementioned options. You can split a large IRA into several smaller ones and name a different beneficiary for each one. If your money is in a company plan, you can roll it into an IRA and then split it. You could name several beneficiaries for one IRA, but then you must use the life expectancy of the oldest beneficiary for the entire IRA, just as when you use a Living Trust as beneficiary. This is especially important if a charity is involved. Remember, it has a life expectancy of zero, so the IRS would consider it the oldest beneficiary. Depending on when you die, this could cause the entire IRA to be paid out in just five years.

Separate IRA's as Beneficiaries

With separate IRA's, one for each beneficiary, you can use each one's life expectancy. This will give you the maximum stretch out over all their ages. It is also fair to the beneficiaries, especially if there is a wide difference in their ages, or if you want to include a charity.

Dividing a Larger IRA as Beneficiary

Dividing a larger IRA depends on your planning decisions. Doing it now, while you are living, is the cleanest approach. If you die first, your surviving spouse can also split your IRA when he or she does a rollover and names new beneficiaries. Under new rules, and under certain circumstances, your IRA can be divided into separate accounts in the year after you die.

Setting up separate IRA's now will make it a little more complicated for you when calculating your required minimum distributions each year, because distributions will have to be calculated for each IRA, but you can take the total of your distributions from any IRA you wish. And it can be well worth the trouble as splitting your IRA like this can also help you save on estate taxes. Any time you name someone other than your spouse as the beneficiary, you need expert advice. You'll need to find an attorney, who is experienced in this area, especially if you have large amounts in these plans. Also, your spouse may need to sign a consent form. Even in non-community property states, spouses now have rights to retirement plans and other benefits.

Beneficiaries for Singles

If you are not married, your decision will be less complicated. You can name any individual, a living trust or a charity as the beneficiary. If you want an individual to receive this money after you die, consider using a Living Trust to keep more control. Before you make a decision, consider all of your options carefully. And make sure your attorney has experience in this area, especially if you have a sizable amount in your tax-deferred plans.

Dying Without a Beneficiary

If you die without a beneficiary, or if you die before your required beginning date, your account must be paid out within five years. If you die after your required beginning date, distributions will be paid over the remaining years of your "fixed life expectancy." This is determined from an IRS table based on your age in the year you die.

Changing a Beneficiary

You can change your beneficiary at any time while you are living and the distributions after you die will be paid over that beneficiary's life expectancy. In fact, now your final beneficiaries do not have to be determined until September 30 of the year after you die, which allows for some clean-up planning to be done after you're gone. For example, your spouse could 'disclaim' some benefits so a grandchild could inherit. No new beneficiaries can be added after you die, so you must have the right beneficiaries named on your account before then.

To change the beneficiary of employer-sponsored plans such as a 401(k), pension, or profit sharing plan, contact your employee benefits or personnel department for the proper form. To change the beneficiary of your IRA or Keogh, you will need to contact the institution where your account is located. Some plans have restrictions on what you can do on the beneficiary designations. Be sure to read the document carefully. If the plan will not let you do what you want to do, consider rolling your money into an IRA as soon as you can. If your money is already in an IRA and the institution will not agree to what you want, consider moving your IRA to another institution.

Roth IRA's

If you qualify, you may want to consider converting some or all of your tax-deferred money to a new Roth IRA. You can only convert from a traditional IRA, so if your money is in a different tax-deferred plan, like a pension or profit sharing plan, you must first roll your money into a traditional IRA and then convert it to a Roth IRA. You will have to pay ordinary income taxes on the amount when you convert.

1. Unlike a traditional IRA that requires you to start taking your money out at 70.5 years of age, with a Roth IRA there are no required minimum distributions during your lifetime. You can leave your money there for as long as you wish.

2. Unlike a traditional IRA, you can continue to make contributions to a Roth IRA after you have reached 70.5 years of age.

3. As a general rule, after five years or 59.5 years of age (whichever is later), all distributions to you and your beneficiaries will be tax-free.

4. You can stretch out a Roth IRA just like a traditional IRA. After you die, distributions can be paid over the actual life expectancy of your beneficiary. Your spouse can even do a spousal rollover and name a new beneficiary. Your tax advisor can help you determine if converting to a Roth IRA would be a good move for you.

Tax-Deferred Annuities

Tax-deferred annuities sold by insurance companies are not IRA's or qualified plans. As a result, they are not governed by the same IRS rules as the plans listed above and the preceding discussion does not apply to them. Before you name a beneficiary, read your contract carefully. There may be some restrictions or income tax issues you need to be aware of when making this decision.

For example, if you are married, naming your spouse as beneficiary may allow the tax-deferred payments to continue over your spouse's lifetime after you die; while naming someone other than your spouse (like your Living Trust) could cause the balance to be paid out all at once after you die. (One solution may be to name your spouse, as first beneficiary and your Living Trust as second beneficiary.)

Estate Taxes

Intended Purpose

The following list of state estate taxes may not be current, but need not be current for its intended purpose. This illustration is designed to show the disparity between estate taxes among the respective states. As with any tax advise, please seek competent counsel in your home jurisdiction.

State Estate Taxes

State	Title or Chapter	Heading
Alabama	Title 40, Section 15 Title 40, Section 15.A	Estate and Inheritance Tax Generation Skipping Transfer Tax
Alaska	Title 43, Chapter 31	Estate Taxes
Arizona	Title 42, Chapter 4	Estate and Generation Skipping Taxes
Arkansas	Title 26, Chapter 59	Estate Taxes
California	California Revenue and Taxation Code: Division 1, Part 10, Chapter 9	Estates, Trusts, Beneficiaries and Decedents
Colorado	Title 39, Article 23 - 24	Estate, Inheritance and Succession Tax

State	Title or Chapter	Heading
Connecticut	Title 12, Chapter 216	Succession and Transfer Taxes
	Title 12, Chapter 216.A	Generation Skipping Transfer Tax
	Title 12, Chapter 217	Estate Tax
	Title 12, Chapter 218	Federal and State Estate Taxes
	Title 12, Chapter 218.A	Estate Income Tax
Delaware	Title 30, Chapter 13	Inheritance
	Title 30, Chapter 14	Gift Tax
	Title 30, Chapter 15	Estate Tax
	Title 30, Chapter 16	Pass-Through Entities, Estates, Trusts
	Title 30, Chapter 17	Interstate Compromise or Arbitration of Death Taxes
District of **C**olumbia	Title 47, Chapter 37	Inheritance and Estate Taxes
Florida	Title XIV, Chapter 198	Estate Taxes
Hawaii	Chapter 48-12	
Idaho	Chapter 236.D	Estate and Transfer Taxes
	Chapter 63-3024	Individual's Tax and Tax on Estates and Trusts
	Chapter 63-3022.L	Individuals who are Officers, Directors, Shareholders, Partners or Members of a Corporation, Partnership or Beneficiaries of a Trust or Estate
Illinois	35 ILCS 405	Illinois Estate and Generation Skipping Transfer Tax Act
Indiana	Title 6, Article 4.1	Death Taxes
Iowa	Title X, Chapter 450	Inheritance Tax
	Title X, Chapter 450.A	Generation Skipping Transfer Tax
	Title X, Chapter 450.B	Qualified Use Inheritance Tax
	Title X, Chapter 451	Iowa Estate Tax
Kansas	Chapter 79, Article 15	Death Taxes
Kentucky	Title XI, Chapter 140	Inheritance Estate Taxes
Louisiana	Title 47, Section 181	Imposition of Tax on Estates and Trusts
Maine	Title 36, Chapters 551 - 575	Inheritance, Succession, Estate Taxes

State	Title or Chapter	Heading
Maryland	Tax-General, Title 7	Death Taxes
Massachusetts	Title IX, Chapter 65	Taxation of Legacies and Successions
	Title IX, Chapter 65.A	Taxation of Transfers of Certain Estates
	Title IX, Chapter 65.B	Settlement of Disputes Respecting the Domicile of Decedents for Death Taxes
	Title IX, Chapter 65.C	Massachusetts Estate Tax
Michigan	Chapters 205.201-205.256	Michigan Estate Tax Act
Minnesota	Chapter 291	Estate Tax
	Chapter 292	Gift Taxes
Mississippi	Title 27, Chapter 292	Gift Taxes
Missouri	Title X, Chapter 145	Estate Tax (formerly Inheritance Tax)
Montana	Chapter 15-30-135	Tax on Beneficiaries or Fiduciaries of Estates or Trusts
	Chapter 15-30-136	Computation of Income of Estates or Trusts (Exemptions)
	Chapter 15-30-137	Determination of Tax of Estates, Trusts
	Chapter 15-30-137	Estates and Trusts Tax Remedies
Nebraska	Chapters 77.2001 - 77.2116	Inheritance Tax, Estate Tax and Generation Skipping Transfer Tax
Nevada	Title 32, Chapter 375.A	Tax on Estates
	Title 32, Chapter 375.B	Generation Skipping Transfer Tax
New Hampshire	Title V, Chapter 87	Taxation of Transfers of Certain Estates
	Title V, Chapter 88.A	Uniform Estate Tax Apportionment Act
	Title V, Chapter 90	Settlement of Disputes Respecting the Domicile of Decedents for Death Taxes
New Jersey	Chapters 58.33 - 58.38	Estate Tax
New Mexico	Chapter 7, Article 7	Estate Tax Generation Skipping Transfer Tax
New York	Tax, Article 26	
	Tax, Article 26.B	Estate Taxes
North Carolina	Chapter 105, Article 1.A	Estate Tax (PDF)
North Dakota	Chapter 57-37.1	

State	Title or Chapter	Heading
Ohio	Title LVII, Chapter 5731	Estate Tax
Oklahoma	Sections 68.801 - 68.827	Inheritance or Transfer Tax
Oregon	Chapter 118	Inheritance Tax
Pennsylvania	Title 20, Chapter 37	Apportionment of Death Taxes
Rhode Island	Chapter 44-22	Estate and Transfer Taxes (Liability and Computation)
	Chapter 44-23	Estate and Transfer Taxes (Enforcement and Collection)
	Chapter 44-23.1	Uniform Estate Tax Apportionment
	Chapter 44-24	Gift Tax
Rhode Island	Title 10, Chapter 40	Imposition, Amount of Inheritance Tax
	Title 10, Chapter 40.A	Estate Tax
	Title 10, Chapter 41	Administration and Collection of Inheritance Tax
South Carolina	Title 12, Chapter 16	Estate Tax
Tennessee	Title 67, Chapter 8	Transfer Taxes
Texas	Tax Code, Sub-Title J, Chapter 211	Inheritance Taxes
Utah	Title 59, Chapter 11	Inheritance Tax Act
Vermont	Title 32, Chapter 185	Interstate Arbitration of Death Taxes
	Title 32, Chapter 187	Interstate Compromise of Death Taxes
	Title 32, Chapter 189	Uniform Estate Tax Apportionment Act
	Title 32, Chapter 190	Estate and Gift Taxes
Virginia	Title 58.1, Chapter 9	Virginia Estate Tax
Washington	Title 83	Estate Taxation